His Special Little Girl

Incest in a Christian Home:
One Child's Story

Jody Lynn Rutherford

PublishAmerica

Baltimore

First printing

ISBN: 1-59286-697-2
PUBLISHED BY PUBLISHAMERICA, LLLP
www.publishamerica.com
Baltimore

Printed in the United States of America

Dedication

From the depths of my heart and soul,
I dedicate my life journey from victim to survivor
to every innocent, priceless child
who has been abused or betrayed,
to those who survived,
to those who didn't,
to those who are still crying out for help.

I also dedicate my story
to my first grandchild,
Grant (Buddy) Alexander Pickett,
who has filled my heart with love and joy beyond all measure.
May he give his heart to Jesus at an early age,
and may the Lord always keep him from harm and evil.

Special Recognition

I give honor and praise to my mother, Barbara, for her
faith,
sense of humor,
integrity,
tenacity,
encouragement,
unconditional love,
and support.

Buddy, Great Grandma Barbie, and Grandma Jody

Acknowledgments

Joe – Loving, kind, patient husband and man of integrity.
Dawn – Precious daughter, friend, and supporter.
Katrina – Special daughter-in-law, friend, and encourager.
Mike and Sharon – Brother-in-law and sister-in-law who purchased a new computer for me so that I could finish my book.
Dee – Godly friend who told me that
"God has appointed you as one of His generals
to help set the children free who are crying out in the darkness."
Elise Meyer – Friend and first editor.
Alice Peppler – Friend and editor.
Michelle Combs, P.A.-C – Friend and physician's assistant.
Dr. Gary Chapman – Associate Pastor, Calvary Baptist Church, Winston-Salem, North Carolina, and
Author of *The Five Love Languages*.
Douglas A. Drossman, MD – Professor of Medicine and Psychiatry, UNC School of Medicine, Chapel Hill, North Carolina.
Rev. Alan D. Wright – Senior Pastor, Reynolda Presbyterian Church, Winston-Salem, North Carolina, and
Author of *Childlike Heart*.
Phil Kelley Jr. – Salem Printing, Winston-Salem, North Carolina
Laura Markland – Sherebiah Photography, Winston-Salem, North Carolina
Betty Smith – Walnut Cove Public Library, Walnut Cove, North Carolina

Table of Contents

Introduction

We appeared to be the all-American Christian family, faithful church members who loved and supported each other. There were six darling, obedient children who were all musicians in the school band programs and the church choir and orchestra. Our handsome father had a steady job, our petite mother baked cupcakes for school parties and sewed doll clothes, and our big dog stood guard.

My siblings and I practiced our musical instruments every day, read our Sunday school lessons each week, and did our homework and chores. We attended church on Sunday morning, Sunday evening, and Wednesday evening, memorized Bible verses, and learned moral standards from our mom. Always together, the endless whirlwind of family activities included: church functions, birthday parties, PTA meetings, Cub Scouts, Girl Scouts, band concerts, music lessons, ball games, bike riding, water skiing, tobogganing, ice skating, paper routes, numerous trips to the grocery store, and countless visits to the pediatrician.

Every house has a story to tell, and the big house at 522 Pipestone Road is no exception. Inside the walls lived a dysfunctional, sad family caused by the evil, demonic spirit of an abusive, controlling, alcoholic father. The sexual, physical, verbal, and emotional abuse that was inflicted on us created an environment of fear, low self-esteem, and rejection. Dad was a master of manipulation. He boasted about being in control of everyone and everything. He charmed everyone he met by literally drawing them into himself and then using them to fulfill his own desires without thinking about the consequences. His religious facade hid what was really going on in our home.

Yet, we loved him very much.

With every possible form of procrastination, the conviction and intensity to write my story became greater. *"I will bless the Lord who counsels me; he gives me wisdom in the night. He tells me what to do. I am always thinking of the Lord; and because he is so near, I never need to stumble or fall" (Psalms 16:7-8)*. There were many sleepless nights as I began to recall tender memories

that had been conveniently and safely tucked away.

Humanly, I didn't feel capable of writing a book. But with God as my partner, I knew I could accomplish anything. Over and over again I repeated, *"The things which are impossible with men are possible with God" (Luke 18:27)*. I had two choices: I could ignore God's compelling voice and remain in denial by putting my childhood behind me, or I could allow Him to use my tormented past as the victim of incest and divorce to help others. Wanting to fulfill God's will in my life more than anything, I humbly and prayerfully endeavored to take the memories from my heart and put them on paper. It took courage, so much courage.

What was it like to be betrayed by someone to whom I looked up to, trusted, and loved? Is it possible to describe the confusion and shame I felt every time Daddy came to my bedroom in the middle of the night, and there, in the black darkness, used me to fulfill his sexual perversion? Is it possible to describe the fear that consumed me when I thought I was pregnant with my dad's baby? And how, how can I possibly put into words the paralyzing anguish and sorrow I have endured? *His Special Little Girl* is a powerful story about growing up in an abusive, dysfunctional home with five siblings, an alcoholic father, and a courageous mother—about steadfast endurance— about desperate attempts to cope with impossible pain—about surviving the devastation of incest and the rejection of divorce—about God's protection and unconditional love and, finally, about the peace of forgiveness and the joy of healing.

Without God and Mom, my siblings and I may not have survived. It takes insurmountable courage to triumph over tough odds and heartbreaking circumstances. In 1990, we made the agonizing decision to have Dad arrested. Contrary to the opinions of some, it was the most courageous, loving thing we could have done.

In order to protect the privacy of others, the names of some of the people in this book have been changed or omitted. This story was not written to be vindictive or judgmental—it was written with a pure motive to give praise and honor to God for his faithfulness, unconditional love, and forgiveness, and to point the way toward help for victims and perpetrators. The graphic abuse scenes were not written to be offensive—they were written with unexaggerated, stark detail so that the reader could feel and experience the heart and soul of an innocent child while being sexually abused.

In the 1960s, incest was considered a private family matter, not a crime, and it was seldom discussed publicly. I don't ever remember hearing the

word incest until I was an adult. When my sister was bleeding from her rectum when she was a little girl, it didn't occur to the pediatrician that she might be a victim of sexual abuse. Physicians didn't recognize the signs of sexual abuse in children, and ministers could hardly accept or fathom that one of their upstanding church members could possibly be molesting a child. Teachers, physicians, and ministers had no legal responsibility regarding abused children. Now, however, they are required to report all child abuse suspicions to the proper authorities immediately.

The very things you read about in this book are happening to our precious children everywhere—in our schools, in our churches, in our doctor's offices, and in our homes and neighborhoods. Even Catholic priests have been and continue to sexually abuse innocent children. Perpetrators are from all walks of life—schoolteachers, ministers, lawyers, physicians, neighbors, friends, and relatives. Many children know and trust their abusers.

The Christian community still does not recognize that incest and pornography are the biggest hidden problems in the church today. I have heard ministers preach about a diverse array of sins from their pulpits: alcoholism, drugs, adultery, gossip, etc. However, they are, quite frankly, and much to my disappointment, reluctant to address the embarrassing, shameful issues of these hidden sins. Although difficult to believe, child abuse is taking place in our church families under the facade of Christianity. For this reason, it is imperative that clergy of all denominations begin addressing this hideous crime. I am proud to say that my pastor, Dr. Wayde Goodall, First Assembly of God, Winston-Salem, North Carolina, recently coordinated "Summit 2003," a seminar on pornography—He is dealing with these hidden sins face-to-face, and God is using him to help protect his congregation and the city of Winston-Salem.

Last year, one of my family members approached their pastor to request an opportunity to share their testimony in church as the survivor of incest. The pastor said he would have to discuss the request with the official church Board. A couple weeks later, he responded by saying that the Board did not feel it was an appropriate subject to talk about from the pulpit. Soon afterwards, I heard the shocking news that the pastor and his son, the youth director, were both fired. The pastor had been taking indecent, sexual liberties with a young female, and his son was involved in homosexual relationships. Knowing that this minister and his son hurt many children is deplorable and heartbreaking, especially when it could and should have been avoided. There are hundreds of similar stories.

Indeed, the time has come for all clergy to denounce these hidden sins—to cause the perpetrators to squirm and repent—to give hope to those who have addictions in these areas—to show the victims where to run for help. Our children deserve to be assured that they are safe, and this assurance should begin in their homes. However, if the adults in their homes don't provide a safe haven for them, then our churches and schools must accept this responsibility. Speaking about the horrendous crime of child sexual abuse from our church pulpits will educate our children and, hopefully, save many from being sexually molested.

Every 15 seconds another innocent child is sexually abused, and most perpetrators have at least 171 victims. The impact of incest is destroying relationships and testing even the strongest commitments—it can literally divide a family. I can testify first-hand, because it nearly ripped my family apart. If our judicial system and society is to come to grips with this repulsive crime that continues to hurt the victims long after the abuse stops, it must be further exposed and the sentencing guidelines for convicted, first-time offenders must be more severe. They are often sentenced to 90 days in jail or five years of probation, a mere slap on the hand considering the magnitude of the crime. Then, many rapists go right out and rape again. The scars and trauma of this attack on innocent children never, ever goes away. Children who are raped don't get a second chance to regain their virginity, and many never recover, so why should the perpetrator get a second, third, and fourth chance?

Survivors must continue to do everything they can to keep this appalling crime foremost in the minds of the American people. When you read the dramatic detail of my abuse and the child abuse facts and statistics at the end of this book, I pray that you are shaken so dramatically that you will want to do everything you can to help end this gruesome and revolting crime.

When my daughter, Dawnie, was a little tot, while she and my mom were driving by a vast field thickly covered with golden dandelions, she said, "Gam! Gam! Daddy says that dandelions are weeds, but you and I both know that they are really flowers!" What a precious observation, filled with such incredible faith. Faith is knowing that we are God's priceless treasures even when we feel utterly worthless. As a victim of incest and divorce, I felt worthless many times. I am so thankful that I had God, who became, and still is, my Heavenly Father. I talk to Him daily as if He is sitting in the same room with me. I know that He will always be there for me and that I can go to Him anytime for love and comfort. And I can confidently entrust Him

with the lives of those who are most valuable to me—my husband, children, and grandson. No child could ask for more.

One

The Beginning

My parents grew up in Benton Harbor near Lake Michigan. Both were victims of dysfunctional childhoods. The abuse in Mom's family started while she was still in her mother's womb. In a drunken rage, her dad would often scream out to his other children, "Come into the bedroom and watch me kill your mother!" One time he bashed Grandma's head in so viciously that she had to be rushed to the hospital. Mom's parents were divorced just before she was born, and her dad changed his last name to Smith and moved away, leaving her mother and six children all alone. Her mother did housecleaning and ironing to provide for her family. They moved constantly, almost every time the rent was due.

Mom had three sisters and two brothers—she was the youngest sibling, affectionately called Bobby Jo. Mom and her youngest brother, Buddy, were the dearest of friends and did just about everything together. When Mom got terrible leg aches when she was a little girl, Buddy would rub her legs for hours while throwing his shoes against the walls to scare the mice away that shared their humble dwelling.

Every Christmas, the Salvation Army brought a basket for Mom and Buddy filled with cranberries, oranges, nuts, and other goodies. They loved the treats, but their eyes always scanned the basket for the two toys they knew would be tucked in somewhere. One year was especially exciting—Mom got a set of royal blue and yellow glass children's dishes and Buddy got a set of Dick Tracy cards. They played cards for hours while Buddy worked 'round the clock to make sure none of the lights on their Christmas tree went out.

For reasons Mom never understood, her oldest sister Dodie disappeared one time and no one knew where she was for many months. But one day, Buddy ran into the house and excitedly proclaimed, "Bobby, oh Bobby, I found out where Dodie is living. Come on, let's go!" They walked and walked, and walked and walked, until Mom's fragile, skinny legs could scarcely hold

her up. After they had walked several miles and Mom began shivering and could go no further, Buddy picked her up and put her into an empty cement dumpster for a few minutes. When he was convinced that she was rested and a little warmer, they walked several more miles. Finally, they arrived. They knocked on the apartment door, and when it opened, they fell into Dodie's arms and cried, "Oh Dodie, Dodie, we found you!" I can only imagine the warm feeling of love that flowed through their bodies at that moment of victory in finding their beloved sister who had eloped.

There was a profound devotion between Mom and Buddy. He was several years older than Mom, and when he got his first job while in high school, he set out on an important venture—to build a bike for her, part by part. One of his friends had an old garage in a nearby alley filled with bicycle parts, and every week when Buddy got paid, he went to this garage and carefully picked out a part—first the frame, then a wheel, then another wheel, then the handlebars, and on and on, until, one by one, he had all the parts to build his little sister's bike. He must have been jubilant and proud when he finally gave her the precious gift. It was the only bike she ever owned, and she cherished it for many years.

Mom loved her grandma and grandpa very much. She and Grandma often had tea parties together.

Dad had three brothers and one sister. When he was only 11 years old, his father and little sister Ellie were hospitalized at the same time. Five-year-old Ellie had a ruptured appendix and wasn't expected to live, and Dad's father was suffering from pernicious anemia. Strangely, his father died and Ellie lived. He was thankful that his sister survived but heartbroken that his father, at age 34, had passed away. His devastation was so great that he put his face in his father's old, worn-out overalls night after night and cried himself to sleep—the smell of his daddy's perspiration on the overalls comforted him. Now his mother was left alone to care for herself and her five children. She took in laundry to support her family, and Dad and his siblings gave her their meager earnings to help financially.

Mom and Dad attended the same high school. In 1943, when they were both 15, Dad was named high school "Pin-Up Boy" and his photograph was displayed in a trophy case in the school hallway. Every time Mom walked by the trophy case, she stopped and stared at the handsome young man. "I've just got to meet him," she sighed dreamily to herself.

Mom was a darling, petite teenager with shoulder-length dark brown hair and beautiful, sparkling blue eyes. She was 5 foot 2 inches and only weighed

17

about 100 pounds. My dad, John Adam, or Johnny as he was called, was strikingly handsome with dark brown hair and brown eyes. He had an extremely masculine build, and all the girls considered him the perfect male specimen. He was in excellent physical condition and several years later was named the Lightweight Golden Glove Boxing Champion of Southwestern Michigan.

Until Mom got her first job, she only had a couple dresses to wear to school, so she was thrilled when one of her friends, a local festival queen, gave her two floor-length dresses. The one she wore to the prom had a red velvet bodice and a red and white polka dot skirt.

While Mom was a teenager, she worked as a soda jerk at Old's Dairy, a local ice cream parlor several blocks from the high school. Mom and the other waitresses used to put a scoop of ice cream in a six-ounce Coke glass, store it under the counter, and take a spoonful every opportunity they got in between customers. When the owner's stepfather visited from Chicago, he always ordered a cherry, pineapple soda and told Mom that she made the best sodas in the world.

Daddy's mother had a boyfriend now, and he went to the dairy every day to buy cream. When he first saw Mom, he went straight home and told Daddy that he had met the cutest little gal he had ever seen. Next thing you know, Daddy found an excuse to visit the dairy so he could ask her out. On their first date, a double date with Daddy's mother and her boyfriend Claude, they went to see *Anchors Away* at the outdoor theater.

Unfortunately, Mom's elation soon turned to doubt and concern. Dad often arrived late for their dates or didn't show up at all. Mom would find out later that some other good-looking female had distracted him on his way to pick her up. One episode was especially heartbreaking. One of her classmates missed cooking class one day, and when she showed up the next day Mom said, "Where were you yesterday?"

"Oh, Barbara," she responded excitedly, "I skipped school and spent the day at the beach with the most gorgeous guy, and now we're going steady."

As giggly and silly as only two teenage girls can get over a boy, Mom said, "Oh, what's his name?"

When her friend said Johnny, Mom's knees went limp. She knew it was her Johnny, and it broke her heart and shattered her dreams.

Mom was confused and hurt and thought a trip to Oklahoma to visit her sister Madeline might help. When she returned from this visit, she broke up with Dad, and he joined the Marines and left home for boot camp.

After a while, Mom began dating someone else. When she received an engagement ring and marriage proposal, Dad's mother found out and wrote Dad a letter. As soon as Dad read the letter, he called Mom and congratulated her, told her he was coming home on a 30-day leave, and asked if she would save him a couple (about 30) days. Mom told him she was no longer engaged. She knew she could never love anyone else but Johnny.

My parents were married in the Annie Banyon Memorial Chapel at the First Congregational Church in Benton Harbor, Michigan on August 15, 1948, where white gladioli were massed at the altar. Mom must have been a lovely sight to behold in her soft ivory ballerina style gabardine suit, pale pink gloves, and dark beige slippers. Her short pink veil was held by an apple blossom band, and she carried a bouquet of pink rosebuds, sweetpeas, and ivy. Dad was equally handsome in his formal Marine dress blues and white gloves. Their mutual friend, Jimmy, sang *Because* and *For You Alone*. There was a reception immediately afterwards for 75 guests at the Tabor home on Britian Avenue. Dinner was served by Mom's sisters, sisters-in-law, and several friends.

Mom was a virgin—she had saved herself for her husband. The pain she experienced caused their marriage consummation to be delayed several days.

By September of 1949, Mom was pregnant with their first child. She was living in Michigan with her mother, and Dad, Private First Class, was stationed in Santa Ana, California. Several weeks before the due date, the doctor discovered that the umbilical cord had strangled the baby and that it was no longer alive. He told Mom that it would be easier and better for her if she could deliver the baby naturally. Jody Lynn was born on June 7, 1949. At that time, new mothers were all in one big hospital ward, and every day the nurses brought the babies in to be breast-fed. All of the other mothers in the ward had babies except Mom. Knowing she would never hold her own precious baby was devastating. Dad returned to Michigan to be by Mom's side when they buried their tiny infant daughter. The loss was overwhelming.

Years later, when Mom and I visited the cemetery where my sister was buried, the loss was still there, in Mom's eyes and in her voice. Jody Lynn didn't have a fancy gravestone, just a simple, flat marker about five inches wide, engraved with a number. They couldn't afford anything else. Even though I knew I would see my sister someday in Heaven, I too felt a profound sense of loss. I wondered what my older sister would have looked like and what musical instrument she would have played. Since none of my siblings played a string instrument, I imagined that she might have played the cello or

violin. Mom eventually made arrangements to have Jody Lynn's name and dates of birth and death engraved on her own tombstone under her name when she is buried. Only a mother would think of something so remarkable.

Soon Mom was expecting again. During Mom's labor, Dad kept telling her that he needed to leave to go see a buddy of his who worked across the street at a gas station. Mom practically had to beg him to stay. John Adam Jr., nicknamed Bumpy, was born on August 11, 1950. He had lots of dark, curly hair and big ears that stuck out and made him look goofy. I was born the following year on July 28, 1951. To preserve their first baby's memory and because they liked the name Jody Lynn so much, my parents named me after my stillborn sister—I was already special. On September 20, 1952, Michael Alan arrived. We called him Tweety Bird, because his huge blue eyes reminded us of the cartoon character.

Dad and his youngest brother Stub were nearly inseparable. When Stub went somewhere with Dad and Mom in their car, he sat in the front seat with Dad and Mom sat in the back—this magnified her lack of self-worth and made her feel even more unimportant. Dad always put his brother first, even before his wife and children. Even though Dad barely made enough money to support his family, he split his paycheck with his brother every week. And then, they'd often go on drinking binges all night and spend their money on beer.

Dad was vicious when he was drunk, almost like a monster. One time when Mom confronted him about his unreasonable allegiance to his brother, he slapped Mom so hard that she momentarily went cross-eyed. It put so much fear in her that she vowed never to mention it again.

After several years of Dad's drinking and uncontrollable rage, Mom had grown weary and didn't think she could handle it any more. Just before their fourth baby was born, she made the decision to seek legal counsel to inquire about her options. When she walked into the attorney's office almost nine months pregnant, the attorney took one look at her and in the most debasing tone of voice said, "Well, by looking at you, there must be something good about your marriage!" Unfortunately, there wasn't much assistance for single parents in the 1950s. Mom paid the attorney $10, went home, packed Dad's clothes and personal belongings in plastic bags and threw the bags outside. But Dad, the master of manipulation, sweet-talked his way back into her life. She kept hoping that he would change.

On November 12, 1953, my bashful brother, Jeffery Raymond, came into the world, followed by Timothy Elliott on June 14, 1957, and my sister,

Tamara Jean, on August 10, 1958.

Six healthy, perfectly formed babies were born in eight years. We favored one another and yet had our own unique personalities. Bumpy, Mike, Timmy, and Tammy had dark brown hair, and Jeff and I had blond hair. All of my brothers had beautiful eyes, and Mike had long, curly eyelashes. And we all had dimples.

I remember Timmy and Tammy coming home from the hospital and once tried to drag Timmy on a receiving blanket to the front door so visitors could see him. He was a dear and sweet baby. And Tammy, delicate and tiny, only weighed 12 pounds when she was one year old.

She was my pride and joy and almost like my very own doll, until she got older, that is, and had to share a bed and bedroom with me!

Mom retained her youthful figure even after being pregnant so many times. With the responsibilities of cooking, cleaning, laundry, and caring for six children and an irresponsible, alcoholic husband, she never stood still long enough to gain any weight.

I was in awe of the love and patience she bestowed on each baby. I was the second oldest and never felt like she loved me less. When I was sick or needed her, I always had her undivided attention.

It never occurred to me how Mom took care of so many children. I guess she just did what she had to do. There were three babies in diapers at the same time—that's a lot of diapers that had to be washed in a ringer washing machine. There were times when Mom had to wash out a diaper by hand and hang it over the oven to dry, and other times when she used a dishtowel for a diaper. It was a happy day when she finally got her first automatic Maytag in 1958.

When one child got sick, the rest got sick, which meant that Mom had the fatiguing job of caring for several children with high fevers at the same time. When this happened, our pediatrician had Mom bring us in through the back door so that we wouldn't infect the other children in the waiting room. I was scared to death of shots and would start crying before we even got into the building. My youngest brother, Timmy, hid behind a chair and would only let his favorite doctor give him a shot.

Dad liked to make babies but didn't want to help take care of them. When one cried too long, Dad would stomp out of the house and stay away as long as he could.

My maternal grandmother, Flossie, was always there to help. Watching her care for each baby brought unique meaning to the word adoration.

I was the first child to have surgery, which I thought made me special. After taking codeine cough syrup for several years because of chronic, severe coughing, our pediatrician scheduled me to have my tonsils removed when I was five years old. On the way to the hospital, Mom took me to the toy store and I picked out a doll dressed in red- and white-striped flannel pajamas and stocking cap. I loved that doll so much that the hair eventually resembled the frizzies. Although I don't remember, Mom said that I began crying for Daddy as soon as the anesthetic wore off. I adored my daddy and knew that I was his special little girl....

Two

My First Home

The two-bedroom, second-story apartment on Catalpa Street in Benton Harbor is my first recollection of a home. I remember several twin beds and cribs in the second bedroom and window fans in the living room. And I can see my little brothers standing up in their cribs. It was here that Bumpy, about four years old, urinated in a glass and tried to coax me to take a drink! Even at that young age, he was already playing pranks on me.

In this apartment, I often tossed Daddy's red and white cigarette packages out of the living room window because I didn't want him to smoke. He would yell at me and then I would turn around and do it again.

I also remember sitting in a chair all alone by the back door in our friend's apartment downstairs. There was a tornado warning, and I was sternly told to sit still and not move from that chair. I couldn't understand where my brothers were and why I was alone. The back door of the apartment was open, and it was dark and windy. I was afraid that the tornado would strike and wanted to cry out, but I knew if I did Daddy would say, "Shut up or I'll give you something to cry about!"

My brothers played in a pile of dirt at the bottom of the back outside stairway—it was their pretend sand box. The yard was filled with lavender, purple, and white lilacs. I was mesmerized by their beauty and would slowly and deliberately inhale their sweet fragrance in order to get the most out of their perfume. I was always let down when the perfectly formed delicate flowers died. I never understood why something so pure and lovely lasted such a short time.

Although I cannot remember, it was in this apartment that Daddy first did something bad to me. I was about 3 or 4 years old. We were in the bathtub together, and he told me to touch his penis. Many years later, he admitted this and asked Mom to forgive him, saying it would never happen again.

She said that if God could forgive him, who was she not to….

23

Three

Memories

In 1958, when I was seven years old, we moved around the corner into the big house at 522 Pipestone Road. After living in a small apartment, this 13-room house seemed like a mansion. Every day Daddy fed big shovels full of black coal into the basement furnace to keep us warm. It wasn't hard for him though, because he had strong, muscular arms.

A giant evergreen stood straight and tall in the front yard, and I was thrilled when I saw that the driveway was lined with lilac bushes—they seemed to be following me. Somewhat run-down steps led up to the front porch, and a black mailbox was attached by the door. I loved the entryway in this house because I knew from watching television that many wealthy families had entryways or foyers in their homes. This small room where we received guests made me feel like my family was rich also.

The first floor had a big living room with bay windows where our Christmas tree stood and a fireplace where our stockings were carefully hung every year—the red, net, plastic Christmas socks with the corners torn from wear, always filled with an orange, a candy cane, and circus peanuts. Oh, the Christmas memories of long ago! My siblings and I would wake up while it was still dark on Christmas morning and tiptoe to each other's rooms and whisper, waiting in anticipation. We had to be quiet so we wouldn't wake Mommy and Daddy up too early. And then, all of a sudden, without warning, one of us would hear a noise downstairs. "Shh! I hear something!" I would then organize the line-up at the bottom of the closed-in, narrow staircase, with one sibling on each step in order from youngest to oldest, and there we'd wait impatiently. The only thing separating us from the magic was a cheap, plastic divider.

And then, with one dramatic movement of his big, strong hand, Daddy would rip open the divider! There, just a few feet in front of us stood the Christmas tree in all its sparkling splendor. On the floor in front of the tree

we could see dolls, toy cars and fire trucks, and the shiny, spectacularly wrapped boxes that Santa had delivered on his sleigh. My eyes quickly darted to the empty glass of milk and cookie plate—indeed, Santa had been there. For a moment, just a moment, we sat in a trance not wanting to break the magical spell. Everyone was happy, I thought to myself—oh how I wish I could keep it this way. I will never forget.

Of course that spell was soon broken with six little brats running, screaming, and ripping holiday paper off the boxes. Although my parents didn't have much money, they tried to give us a good Christmas. One of my favorite Christmas gifts was a Polly Doll with doll clothes that were handmade by my mom and much nicer than any I had ever seen in the toy stores. It didn't matter that all my friends had Barbie Dolls, because Polly looked just like a Barbie to me.

Mom spent hours and hours making Christmas sugar cookies for us—the kind where the dough had to be rolled out with a rolling pin and tediously cut out with all the different shaped cookie cutters, then covered with frostings of all colors, and finally, creatively and painstakingly decorated with a variety of sugar sprinkles. Sometimes we helped her decorate, and toward the end we'd get silly and start tossing the sprinkles—then the kitchen floor made a crunchy sound when we walked on it.

The dining room had a rectangular-shaped oak table and iron chairs that were covered with stiff gold- and brown-striped plastic fabric. Also in the dining room was an enormous, old upright piano that Dad purchased for $75. I loved that piano and practiced it every day. I can still see two pieces of music sitting on it like it was yesterday—*Moon River* and *On Life's Highway*. I performed *Moon River* at one of my first recitals and *On Life's Highway* for my first piano offertory in church. Mom wanted me to have a new dress for this special occasion but didn't feel well, so she gave Aunt Karen $10 and asked her to take me shopping.

While I played *On Life's Highway*, Daddy read the words. Although torn and yellow from age, I still have this piece of music and play it occasionally. The memories pull on the tender places of my heart. I wonder if Daddy remembers the words.

On Life's Highway

Far away from any road,
Where no passerby can see,

25

Roams my heart in solitude,
On life's highway, God, with Thee;
Knowing, when all else doth fail,
Thy compassion shall prevail.
Father, with Thee, Let me be,
On life's highway, God, with Thee.

Oft-times clouded is the ray
That tow'rd Heaven beckons me;
Oft my wand'ring heart is lured
On some by-path, far from Thee.
Father, when my footsteps stray,
Guide me back into Thy way.
Father, with Thee, Let me be,
On life's highway, God, with Thee.

—Words & Music by Bertrand-Brown
The Willis Music Company, Cincinnati, Ohio

Off the dining room through French doors was an old screened-in side porch. I never figured out how the nasty flies always seemed to find their way into the torn places of the screen—it annoyed me so much that I covered the holes with masking tape and the screen soon resembled a patchwork quilt. Every spring, I waited in anticipation for the temperature to get warm enough so I could clean the porch. Grandma Flossie had coloring contests out there for the neighborhood children and us, and I spent hours out there in the old wicker, losing myself in Nancy Drew mysteries.

A kitchen should be a warm, happy place filled with the chatter of sharing activities and ideas at the end of busy days while eating the evening meals, a secure place where children openly express their feelings and parents praise their accomplishments. But this wasn't so in our kitchen. We weren't allowed to talk during mealtime. "You are to be seen and not heard," Daddy constantly reminded us. We knew not to utter a peep. Although I understand the probability of chaos, it would have been nice if Daddy had allowed us to take turns talking. Instead, his controlling, obnoxious attitude during meal times created a demeaning, fearful atmosphere that affected my already nervous digestive system.

In this kitchen during an argument with Mom one time, I threw a hand

mirror across the floor and it shattered. While I was sassing her, Daddy walked in and slapped me across the face, so forcefully that I thought I might not ever see straight again. It stunned me into silence. I shouldn't have been sassing her and needed to be punished, but being slapped so hard that it left Daddy's handprint on my cheek seemed obsessive.

The kitchen had an old-fashioned walk-in pantry lined with neatly organized blue and white Currier and Ives dishes—I licked and stuck hundreds of S&H green stamps onto the Kroger grocery store forms so that Mom could get the whole set of dishes. We were lucky, because Daddy always got lots of stamps when he fueled his semi. The pantry also had empty juice glasses that had once been filled with Kraft cheese, pots and pans, and sometimes, cookies and potato chips. Snacks were located on the third shelf on the right-hand side, and because I was usually the one who put the clean dishes away, I frequently snitched a cookie or handful of chips. We couldn't afford many snack foods or lunchmeat, so we had to use our imaginations. Two of my favorite snacks were butter and brown sugar on white bread and homemade frosting on graham crackers. I made sandwiches with radishes, mayonnaise, salt and pepper, and when I took them out of my lunch bag at school and saw the other kid's bologna sandwiches, I turned red with embarrassment. Mom spent insurmountable hours preparing delicious, homemade meals and desserts for us. My favorites were: bean soup, chili, corn bread, meatloaf, mashed potatoes, coleslaw, kidney bean salad, macaroni and cheese, banana cake, and strawberry shortcake with hot biscuits right from the oven, freshly picked strawberries, and homemade whipping cream.

When we had hot dogs for dinner, my youngest brother Timmy always cut his into tiny pieces. When I asked him why, he said, "Because when there's lots of pieces it looks like I have more than one hot dog." Although I don't ever remember going hungry, I know there were many times when Mom didn't have enough money to buy food.

Dishes, dishes, and more dishes! My siblings and I took turns washing the dinner dishes, and when it was my week, I began clearing the table almost before Daddy took his last bite so that I could get outside to play faster. Doing dishes for eight was an awful, time-consuming chore. Sometimes I felt sorry for my brothers and offered to do the dishes for them during their week. "What was it like not having a dishwasher?" I asked Mom years later. "Why did I need a dishwasher?" she laughed. "I had six!"

There were two additional rooms on the first floor. One was used as my parents' bedroom and the other as a laundry/play room. The laundry/play

room had old gray, speckled linoleum that curled up at the edges. Here, Mom stood for hours at the ironing board wearing faded cut-off blue jean shorts rolled up at the cuffs several times, a green and white gingham-checked sleeveless shirt, and soiled tennis shoes that had holes in the toes. She wore these clothes almost every day during the warm weather.

Next door was a small bathroom, which I took pride in scrubbing. I was relieved that the window had a shade, because I was always afraid that Daddy or one of my brothers would stand outside and spy on me while I took my baths.

A narrow, closed-in staircase led to the second floor with four bedrooms and one bathroom.

Every child should experience the joy of grandparents, and my Grandma Flossie brings back wonderful memories. For a few years, she used two of the upstairs rooms, one for her bedroom and one for her living room. She looked like a movie star. She never went out of the house without wearing a hat and white gloves. My siblings and I took turns spending the night with her and sleeping in her big bed. When it was my turn, Grandma and I would talk long into the night. She dyed her beautiful hair a grayish-blue color, and the color often came off on her pillow, which made me laugh. There were lots of wonderful things in Grandma's bedroom which she let me explore—jewelry, hatpins, books, cards, fancy hats, gloves, makeup, and perfume in delicately-shaped bottles.

She worked at a dry cleaning business on Pipestone Road, and sometimes I got to go to work with her. Together, hand-in-hand, we walked the eight blocks. It was a long walk for a little gal, but I didn't mind because I was with my grandma. When I got tired, I curled up under the counter and took a nap. When I got bored, I hooked the safety pins together until they resembled a long train. Grandma almost always bought me a small bag of candy on the way home. My favorites were coconut bon-bons, and I made sure that the nice lady behind the counter put every color in my bag—white, yellow, pink, and brown.

I knew that I was special to Grandma and that she loved me very much. She never grew weary of my company. One of my greatest treasures is "black sambo," the little doll that she made for me out of black yarn.

Because Daddy spent most of his check on beer for himself and his brother, Mom often ran out of necessities. There were many times when Mom would hesitantly call Grandma and say, "Mom, I'm out of milk for the babies," or "I need to borrow 50 cents." Grandma's kind response was always the same.

"Well, just let me get up and get dressed and I'll be right over," she would say. Then she would show up with milk, bread, a couple potatoes, and sometimes bacon. I never heard Mom or Grandma complain.

After Grandma died, Tammy and I shared the big bedroom at the top of the stairs on the right. This is when we made up the words "doobies" and "nibber" for our breasts and vaginas. We slept in a full-size bed together and enjoyed looking out the window late at night during the warm months. Sometimes we would see a man staggering down the sidewalk late at night, and I wondered if he had been drinking at the same bar as Daddy.

I wasn't as close to my paternal grandmother, Crystal, although she was nice to me. Sometimes Bumpy and I went with her to swim at Lake Michigan's Rocky Gap Park, and on the way she would buy poppy seed rolls from the bakery where she worked. We didn't like poppy seed rolls, but instead of telling her, we threw them out the window and pretended that we had eaten them.

One time when she was screaming from excruciating pain caused from impacted bowels, of which I knew nothing about, Mom came to her rescue by giving her a suppository and helping her get to the toilet. After her bowel problem, I began wondering if the same thing was causing the pain in my stomach and rectum. I either had diarrhea or constipation and seldom went number two without pain. The diarrhea made me weak and chilled. The constipation forced me to strain and push as hard as I could to get the hard poopoo out, and afterwards, it would hurt and blood would come out of my rectum. I was too embarrassed to tell Mommy.

Daddy checked the doors every night to make sure they were locked, or at least this is what he told Mommy he was doing. Then he'd tiptoe to my bedroom in the blackness of the night like a thief, move his fingers back and forth in my nibber, and then wrap a wad of Kleenex around the end of his pee pee. Before he left my bedroom, he reassured me that only special little girls did this with their daddies. I wasn't afraid, because it felt good, sort of like when Mommy tickled my back. And I felt special, because I knew it was mine and Daddy's secret.

Our house didn't have air conditioning, and sometimes it was so hot in the summer that I had to peel myself from the sheets. The only respite from the heat was when my siblings and I got to run through the sprinkler or go to the beach. During the winter, no matter how badly I had to go to the bathroom at night, I would hold it. It was so cold in my bedroom that I could see my breath, and I didn't want to leave the warm cocoon that my body heat had

formed in my bed. When I got thirsty, all I had to do was scrape ice from the windowsill with my fingernails.

There was a big Catholic Church and school in our neighborhood. I wanted to go to school there because the girls wore cool uniforms—pleated plaid skirts and white blouses. But we weren't Catholic, so we had to go to Calvin Britain Grade School on Britain Avenue. It was only a six-block walk, but with our undersized legs it seemed like a long way, especially in the cold, winter months when the blizzards blinded you and the temperatures dipped into the low teens. When it was really cold, our nostrils stuck together and our boots made a crunchy sound as we walked on the packed-down ice and snow. I often walked with my fingers intertwined in the belt loops of Bumpy's jeans so that I could keep up. Even though we didn't have much money, Mom made sure we had warm coats, hats, mittens and boots. My brothers wore those silly looking over-the-shoe rubber boots with the buckles.

The light brick school building had shiny hallway floors that always looked like they were freshly waxed, finger paintings and construction paper artwork on the walls, and a big principal's office where my brothers were often sent for misbehaving. Mike was a good artist, so his pictures were often displayed on the walls. I was proud of him and made sure that everyone knew he was my brother. The playground had a great swing set, and during recess my friend Kathy and I pumped our legs on the swings until we went so high we felt like we were soaring. The higher we went, the louder we sang *Puff the Magic Dragon*. We had no idea what the words of the song meant, we just liked the tune. When I could go no higher, I pretended that an angel's strong arms were carrying me all over the beautiful soft blue sky, high above anyone or anything that could hurt me. Those were some of my happiest times.

The cold milk that was delivered to the school every day in the miniature glass bottles with the foil caps was thirst quenching, and we always had cookies to go with our milk.

I don't remember many of my teachers, but I remember enjoying school and doing really well. Good grades didn't come quite as easy for my brothers though. They were slow readers, and didn't always retain what they read. I felt sorry for them and tried to help them with their homework, although sometimes my patience dwindled. When they got older, last-minute requests to do book reports was especially frustrating, but of course I didn't do it for free—they had to pay me, even if only 25 cents!

I was a Brownie and Girl Scout in grade school and wore the uniforms and badges with honor and pride. One year I sold the most Girl Scout cookies,

and that was when they were sold door-to-door. In one of the scout programs, my participation was to give a reading. But just before I went on stage, Daddy sternly reprimanded me in front of everyone. I don't remember what I did, but I know I cried so hard that I could barely get through the poem. Mom was furious with Dad, and they argued about it all the way home. She told him that it was completely unnecessary. He probably told her to shut up and mind her own business.

Several of my brothers were in Cub Scouts, and one year Daddy helped Bumpy build a car for the Soap Box Derby Race. His car was black with white trim, and even though it didn't win the race, I was still proud of him. It's one of the few times that Daddy did something special with Bumpy.

Sometimes Mom let us walk to Connaly's Drug Store to buy penny candy. The curved, glass front candy counter made it easy to see all the yummy delights—licorice, Lic-a-Maid, Bazooka Bubble Gum, Tootsie Rolls, Mary Janes, etc. I liked the cartoons that came in the Bazooka gum wrappers, and root beer popsicles were another favorite. Spears Grocery Store was located next door, and this is where Mom did most of the grocery shopping. As with other families back then, Mom often called her order in on the telephone and had it delivered to our house. The employees at Spears got excited when she called, because the food on her grocery list was so organized that it coincided with the aisles. Perhaps this is where I got my organizational skills.

One of my happiest memories as a little girl were the times when Daddy took all of us to the big snow-covered hill at Twin City Containers where he worked. We'd slide down the hill on waxed cardboard boxes that Daddy flattened out—waxed cardboard was really slick on the snow, making us fly down the hill so fast that sometimes we'd almost make it to the train tracks—such a happy memory!

Four

Oral Sex with Daddy

I'm about eight years old now. I can hear several of my brothers playing baseball outside one afternoon. As the warm summer breeze awakens the lilacs, their delicate fragrance begins to drift into the open windows of my bedroom—the lilacs are laughing. After finishing my book about Shirley Temple, I begin to feel sleepy and close my eyes. When I'm almost asleep, Daddy shakes me back to reality. "Shh," he whispers. "You and Daddy are going to do something different today." I'm surprised, because he has never come to my bedroom in the light. Where is Mom? I wonder.

I am on my back, and Daddy's 200-pound body is straddling my petite frame. He pulls his pee pee out of his thin, white boxer shorts—it looks limp like a thirsty flower that hasn't been watered in a long time. He dangles it back and forth over my closed mouth. The odor of it is peculiar, and something is oozing out of the little hole at the end. To cope with the yucky feeling in my stomach, I close my eyes and try to concentrate on the sweet smell of the lilacs.

He tells me to open my mouth and suck on it. No longer small and limp, it is getting bigger and bigger. With his strong hands, he holds my head and mouth. The more I struggle to pull away, the farther he forces his pee pee into my throat. I gag and feel like I'm going to throw up, but he continues to push it back and forth in my mouth.

For a second, I manage to turn my head and his pee pee flops out of my mouth. "Stop, Daddy, I can't breathe. Please stop. My mouth hurts!" He pushes it back into my mouth even though my jaws ache. "I'm almost done," he murmurs breathlessly. All of a sudden, my mouth is filled with warm, thick liquid. I cannot move because his hands on my head are too strong. I am forced to swallow.

He is off me now. His pee pee is still big, and I wonder how long it takes to shrink. He tucks it into his boxer shorts and leaves abruptly without saying

anything.

I don't like this new thing that Daddy made me do to him. It makes me feel naughty.

I am dizzy and sick to my stomach.

I am so thirsty.

My mouth is closed, but it still feels like it's open.

I feel icky.

But I'm Daddy's special little girl.

It was so long ago, and yet, I remember….

Five

Sunday School

Shortly after we moved to 522 Pipestone Road, Mom began sending us to First Assembly of God's Sunday school on Cherry Street. Every Sunday without fail, she got up while it was still dark outside and took on the daunting challenge of getting Bumpy, Mike, Jeff, and me ready. Timmy and Tammy were still too young to go. When Tammy got a little older and started going with us, I fixed her hair with those plastic animal-shaped barrettes. It was a tough job getting the part straight, but I knew it saved Mom a lot of time.

My parents didn't want anything to do with religion, but they willingly sent us to Sunday school. I'm not sure if they sent us to get us out of their hair for a couple hours or because they knew we enjoyed it. Whatever the reason, we were enthusiastic. I was especially happy at Sunday school, because I knew Daddy couldn't do anything to me while I was there.

The big church bus pulled up to the curb and Mom waved good-bye to us as we ran to get on. The drivers were always nice, and they never treated us any differently than the other children even though they knew we were poor.

The other children made fun of us and nicknamed us pixies. I never knew why—because we were poor maybe, or because we were bus kids. All of our Sunday school teachers were kind, especially Mr. and Mrs. Emde. How they tolerated my naughty brothers with their cowlicked hair, I will never know. Picture it—four boys acting like boys, running in all different directions. The Emdes were firm and had to spank my brothers several times, but they never stayed angry. Just like Jesus, they loved us, and loved us, and loved us some more.

In Sunday school we sang choruses—my favorites were *Deep and Wide*, *Jesus Loves Me*, *Father Abraham*, and *This Little Light of Mine*. We also listened to Bible stories, made arts and crafts, and drew pictures using big boxes of crayons filled with hundreds of colors. I only had eight colors at home, so coloring was especially exciting. We always had juice and cookies,

and, as usual, I couldn't wait for snack time! All too soon, Sunday school would be over and our stubby legs would once again climb the big steps to board the bus. I held tightly to the Bible verses I had received and the pictures I had drawn, sometimes so tightly that they became crumpled. I wanted to proudly display them for Mommy and Daddy when I got home.

The most important thing I learned in Sunday school was that God was my Father in heaven. Wow, I thought—I'm special because I have two daddies, one at home and one in heaven.

Mom made some of my dresses and sometimes made a matching drawstring purse. I particularly remember one Easter outfit—a white dress with yellow flocked flowers, a matching purse, a straw hat, white gloves, lacy white anklets and black patent leather shoes. Back then, little girls and ladies always wore white gloves (or "party mittens" as one of my precious nieces used to call them).

Shortly after I turned ten, Daddy told me I was his big girl now and that he wanted to do something with me that was really special. This is when he started putting his penis inside my nibber. Sometimes he put something on his penis that he called a rubber, and it was slimy at the end. "Only special big girls get to do this with their daddies," he whispered as he kissed my not-yet-developed dubies. When he pushed his big penis inside me, it hurt and I told him that it hurt. "If you just relax it will feel good and won't hurt so much," he reassured me. But it continued to hurt long afterwards, and sometimes even walking was uncomfortable.

Again, Daddy told me I was special and that we must always keep our secret, firmly and resolutely persuading me to promise never to tell anyone. Daddy was very handsome, and the aftershave he wore made him smell so good. I trusted him and was determined to do everything I could to please him, and after a while it didn't hurt as much.

I was confused though and afraid of Daddy's temper, and I couldn't understand why he had to sneak to my bedroom late at night after it was dark and everyone was sleeping. When I asked him he always had the same answer: "Because it's a secret."

Mike had a tiny bedroom right across from mine, and once, in the middle of the night, I got on top of him and pretended to do what Daddy was doing to me. I had my panties and pajamas on though, and I don't think Mike even remembers.

During the hot weather, Daddy often made my brothers strip and line up in the back yard, and then he'd shave their heads and take a bar of soap and

the garden hose and scrub them down. I suppose he thought he was helping Mom, but I didn't think it was very nice. If he ever tried to add me to that line-up, I thought to myself, I'd run away.

My siblings and I took turns going on long-distance trips with Daddy in his shiny new 18-wheeler. It was exciting getting up before the birdies in the early morning hours while it was still dark outside. These trips were sometimes long and boring, but it was worth it just to get to eat in the restaurants and sleep and watch television in the bunk of the tractor. For some reason, Daddy never did anything to me in his truck. I felt important when I looked out the window from the passenger seat down at all the people in their cars. "My daddy is the best truck driver in the whole world," I would tell everyone melodramatically. "His CB handle is Dutchman." I didn't like coffee, and Mom thought I was too young to have it, but I always got a cup for breakfast just like Daddy. "She'll have half and half," he'd tell the waitress with a wink and a smile. Half and half was part coffee and part cream. Daddy always let me pick out a toy at the truck stops and always bought me Juicy Fruit Gum. I would chew one stick of gum and take the rest home to my brothers. And he never returned home without a trinket for Mom.

In late 1959, Daddy's oldest brother Don and his wife and family came to visit us. It was during this visit that my cousin Crystal and I laughed so hard that we wet our pants and it dripped down onto the rug in my bedroom. We loved to laugh together. She was a lot taller than me and called me "little sister."

Uncle Don was an Assembly of God minister in Rupert, Idaho. He had been invited to be a guest preacher at our small church and had planned to do a skit as part of his sermon.

Although my parents weren't attending church, Daddy agreed to be in his brother's skit. I was very surprised that he agreed to go to church, let alone participate in something. He was supposed to walk down the middle aisle in a stooped position carrying a big, heavy-looking burlap sack. The words SIN and BURDENS were printed on the sack. To my astonishment, he began to cry while he walked down the aisle as the piano softly played *There's Room at the Cross*. When he got to the altar, he dropped the bag of sins and burdens, knelt down, and continued to cry. He cried so hard that his shoulders shook. As a broken man, perhaps realizing that his only hope was in the Cross, he asked God to forgive him and come into his heart. It was December 29, 1959. I was eight years old.

That same day, I overheard Daddy talking to Mom. He confessed to her

that he had made me touch his private parts one time several years ago and that he had been involved in an adulterous affair. He told Mom he had given his heart to Jesus, and he asked her to forgive him. She said that if God could forgive him, so could she. I knew lying was a sin, so it was confusing when Daddy didn't tell her the whole truth. This is when I figured out why Daddy usually came to my bedroom in the night. It wasn't because I was special. It was because he couldn't take a chance that someone might catch him. From that time on, I no longer thought Daddy was so wonderful.

But I knew God could change the worst sinner. I had learned this in Sunday school. During the next few months, Daddy did change. He didn't drink as much, he was home more, and his temper wasn't near as volatile. Seeing this change in him encouraged Mom and gave her hope, and in April 1960, she gave her heart to Jesus.

Finally, I wouldn't have to ride on the bus anymore and we'd all go to church together with our parents like the other families. It didn't matter that we would be driving to church in a broken-down 1951 Chevy Suburban that had a big hole in the floor, because we would be going all together as a family. We used to watch the road fly by through that hole, and once in a while if we thought we could get away with it, we threw something out of the hole. Then we'd have to hide our laughter so Daddy wouldn't find out.

Soon afterwards, my parents joined the church choir. In 1962, a new church was built on Nickerson Avenue. This is where all of my siblings and I asked Jesus to come into our hearts and were dedicated and eventually baptized.

For a while, Daddy stopped coming to my bedroom at night. In my innocent mind, I didn't think he would drink or put his penis inside me anymore because now he was a Christian. I didn't understand that God gives us our own will. He would do real well for several months, and then all of a sudden he would go on a rampage, stay out all night drinking, coming home drunk, and then molesting me. Sometimes I would tell him no and he would go away. He drank so much that I could smell the alcohol on his breath and when the sweat oozed out of his pores. One night he was so drunk that he made himself a sandwich out of dog food—he thought it was corn beef hash.

Every time he would backslide, he would stand up in church the following week and ask the congregation and God to forgive him. On one hand, Daddy cried and seemed to be sorry. On the other, he continued to abuse me and beat my brothers with his leather belt. The emotional contradiction was baffling. No one, absolutely no one knew what was really going on in our home, not even Mom. Daddy was a good actor, and he made sure there were

no signs.

On Saturday mornings, we watched cartoons. Some of my favorites were *Bugs Bunny, Road Runner, Mickey Mouse,* and *The Flinstones.* We also enjoyed *Leave It To Beaver, The Donna Reed Show, Dennis the Menace, I Love Lucy,* and *Lassie.* And over and over and over again, Mom read our favorite book with the fuzzy critter, *Winkie Bear.*

On Friday or Saturday evenings, sometimes Daddy made popcorn, dressed my siblings and me in our pajamas, loaded us into the back of the station wagon that we now owned, and took us all to the outdoor, drive-in theater. We were accustomed to going to bed every evening around 8:30, so we never stayed awake very long. I can't remember the name of one movie, but it was still an adventure.

During the early evenings in the spring and summer months, a favorite outdoors game was tin can alley. The person who was it had to kick an empty can, then count to 100 while everyone else was hiding. Then they had to search for us, and when they spotted us, we had to race to home, get there before they did, and kick the can and shout "tin can alley!" It was lots of fun inventing new hiding places. Red Rover was another popular neighborhood game, but I was so small I was never able to break through the linked arms of the opposing team when they screamed, "Red Rover, Red Rover, send Jody right over!" Daddy often took us for long rides in the country and bought us ice cream cones. Daddy's and my favorite flavor was butter pecan.

Other neighborhood activities included: hop scotch, hoola hoops, double Dutch jump rope, Simon Says, and marbles. The black girls at my school were especially good at double Dutch jump roping. When I finally mastered the art of jumping into the double ropes, I felt like I had conquered the world. I soon became as good as my black friends.

I watched every Shirley Temple movie over and over again and spent hours playing with my Shirley Temple doll and Lennon Sister and McGuire Sister paper dolls. Jacks was my favorite game, and Mom got on the floor and played with me often—onsie, twosies, threesies, etc., and then, with one theatrical motion of her delicate hand, she would scrape up all six jacks and catch the ball before it bounced again! She was good. She was really good. If Jacks had been an Olympic event, she surely would have won a medal.

Trick-or-treat! My siblings and I waited impatiently for Halloween every year, because Halloween meant free candy. We had to be creative and come up with our own unique ideas for costumes. It seemed that we always scurried around at the last minute, so there were lots of on-the-spot groveling for

Mom to find bandanas, the perfect hat or jewelry, to darken our eyebrows with coal or apply rouge and lipstick, or to stuff our shirts to make it look like we had big boobs. Back then, parents didn't worry about their children walking around the neighborhood to trick or treat. Our favorite house to visit was our next-door neighbors', because they always gave out the biggest candy bars. When we were done trick-or-treating, we had to dump all of our candy out on the living floor so Mommy and Daddy could inspect it. Daddy usually took the best candy bars, leaving us the apples, suckers, and gum. This made me mad, and I told him that he should dress up and go out and get his own candy!

In the winter, we spent hours at the skating rinks in Benton Harbor and St. Joseph. For Christmas one year, I got a new pair of white figure skates. Now I was really cool. Once in a while I would hold hands with one of the boys I knew, and we would skate around and around the rink together in rhythm to some romantic tune. We'd wait to go into the warming house until our feet were so cold they were stiff and itchy.

Entertainment after holiday meals, especially Thanksgiving, became a family tradition, complete with hand-written programs made with crayons by Tammy. Daddy was almost always the emcee for these programs. Several would sing or play their instruments, one or two would tell a joke, and Tammy would usually recite a poem. I felt proud when I played my flute, and even at that young age considered it a serious performance. When aunts, uncles, and cousins joined us for a holiday dinner, they also participated.

Daddy and I carved the turkey together every year, sampling as we went along. I always got the wishbone, and after carefully rinsing it off and hanging it to dry, I would solemnly make my wish!

Saturday evening was popcorn night. Daddy made it the old-fashioned way by shaking the big pan over the burner on the stove, melting real butter, and adding lots of salt. No one could make popcorn like Daddy. He made such a big batch that he had to put it in a canner. Sometimes he would send one of us across the street to Talbott's Drug Store to get star chocolates and Nehi pop to go with our popcorn. We each got to choose our own flavor, and the eight-pack we brought back looked colorful with the red, orange, green, purple, and brown bottles. My favorite was red pop. Daddy also sat for hours and peeled red Delicious apples for us. They always tasted better without the skins.

Once in a while we'd go to McDonald's. Although I looked forward to these rare occasions, I dreaded it when I got in high school. Some of my

friends worked at McDonald's, and I wanted to hide my face in embarrassment when they packed all that food into the big cardboard box that resembled a two-story house. Our orders ultimately exceeded the capacity of the bags made for average-sized family orders. Because of the cost, we were each only allowed to have one hamburger and one bag of fries. If one of my brothers were still hungry, I would pretend that I was full and give them the rest of my fries or the last couple bites of my burger. (When my husband reads this he won't believe it because he knows how much I love to eat.) When the boys got older, Dad let them order two burgers.

And Capozio's pizza night—how can I describe the aroma and taste of the most delicious pizza in the world, mouth-watering and scrumptious, usually ordered with pepperoni, mushrooms, and green pepper? Umm! I can almost taste it. They were so good that if Mom or Dad drew one of my aunt's or uncle's names at Christmas time, they would buy a half-baked Capozio's pizza, give it to the person whose name they drew, and then that lucky recipient would simply have to finish baking their pizza at home.

Just as many farm families ring a bell, Dad had his own unique way of getting our attention. He would put his thumb and pointer finger in his mouth between his upper and lower teeth and let out a shrill, pierce whistle. The entire neighborhood soon recognized that whistle. "That's John calling his kids!" they'd say. When we heard that whistle, we knew we better run home as fast as we could. The older I got, the more humiliated I felt when I heard the sound of his whistle. It made me feel like a dog!

Getting a new dress or pair of shoes was about the most exciting thing that could happen. One year, Mom bought me a beautiful new dress for Easter and I carefully hung it in my closet. It was made out of white, delicate voile fabric and had long, puffy sleeves. I was so excited about wearing it to church on Easter Sunday that I could barely sleep. I went to my closet every day to look at my dress. But one day, I noticed a strange odor, like smoke. When I opened the closet door and pulled my dress out, I couldn't believe my eyes. An unsightly hole, about two inches long, had been burnt out of one of the sleeves. I screamed for Mom, and she came running up the stairs. "There's a hole in my dress, Mom, and it's ruined. My beautiful dress is ruined!" After questioning my brothers, we discovered that Timmy had lit a match in his bedroom and stuck it through a hole that joined our closets. Normally I hated it when my brothers got the belt, but this time Timmy deserved to be punished. Mom came to the rescue and found a seamstress who mended the sleeve so that you could hardly tell it had been burnt.

When I woke up on Easter Sunday and found my Easter basket on the floor next to my bed filled with marshmallow chicks, hollow chocolate bunnies (that cheap waxy chocolate), malted milk eggs, and jelly beans, and saw my dress hanging in the closet, I prayed that the happiness I felt would last forever.

I made myself smile, but the carefree grin, plastered to my face like a mask, covered up the despondent, pathetic little girl with the long pigtails. The fun, happy times of my childhood were spoiled by the constant fear that Daddy was going to make me do awful, sickening things to him. It's like he took the happy times away from me—all of them....

Six

Death, Sickness, and Sexual Abuse

In the spring of 1960, Grandma Flossie was supposed to have surgery for the repair of a fallen womb. One Sunday evening, she asked Mom to stay home from church so they could go over some important papers together. I couldn't believe it when Mom asked Dad if she could stay home, because Dad never, ever allowed any of us to miss church. He didn't give in easily this time either, and he ranted and raved, but Mom persisted and stayed home with Grandma.

That evening, Mom noticed that Grandma's skin had a yellow cast to it, so yellow in fact, that she called the doctor the following day and was told to bring Grandma in right away. The doctor took one look at her and knew that something was terribly wrong and that he wouldn't be able to perform the scheduled surgery. During exploratory surgery that same week, a malignant tumor the size of an orange was found in her liver. The surgeon told Mom that Grandma probably wouldn't live more than a few months. She passed away six weeks later.

Just before she died, she told Mom she wanted to see her babies. So Mom cleaned us all up and took us to the hospital so Grandma could see us one last time. Tammy, not quite two years old, stood at the foot of Grandma's hospital bed. When Grandma saw us, she said, "Oh, I've just been dying...!" What she meant was, "I've just been dying to see my babies." She didn't know she would soon be leaving.

I was sitting in the dining room when Mom told us that Grandma was in heaven. A big lump immediately grew in my throat. I thought Grandma Flossie would always be there for us and didn't know if we could make it without her. She filled a place in my sensitive heart that only a grandma could fill, and I know she would have helped me through the tough times. My life was never the same after she went away.

When she died, it was too much for Mom. Already deeply depressed, this

unexpected tragedy pushed her into a complete nervous breakdown. Her gynecologist, the same physician who delivered my siblings and later my son, said he saw it coming for years. Another physician treating Mom felt that her nervous breakdown was the result of an alcoholic husband and a dominating mother-in-law. Although I never saw much endearment between the two, Mom always treated Grandma Belcher with respect, and I am quite certain that Grandma Belcher loved Mom. It must have been awkward for Grandma to watch her own son mistreat his wife and children.

I believe that the strain on Mom's body, caused from having so many children so close together, along with all of the other stress she had to endure for so many years, finally took its toll. Dad was so involved in his own selfish agenda that he hadn't noticed Mom slipping into this serious illness.

In the early months of 1962, I noticed that Mom was crying a lot and didn't have any appetite or energy. I didn't understand why, and it scared me. I had no way of knowing that she was suffering from a mental disease. When you're young, you think your Mom will always be there for you and that she will never die. She became so weak that she couldn't even swallow soup and Dad had to give her a bath. He finally called the doctor and was told that they could see Mom in six weeks. The nurse told him to bring her in immediately after Dad aggressively explained that Mom wouldn't make it six more weeks.

From 1962 to 1964, Mom was admitted into the hospital several times. When she was home, I took peanut butter toast and tea to her when she was in bed. She lived in her bed most of the time. I cried myself to sleep many nights, because I thought she was going to die.

Mom was taking prescribed sleeping pills and the powerful sedative Thorazine, and she was often in another world. These necessary drugs, combined with the fact that we lived in a huge house, make it easy to understand why Mom didn't know what Dad was doing to me. When she went to sleep, she was out, and that's usually when he would sneak up to my room.

My siblings and I argued all the time. Mom called it bickering. Although it's normal for brothers and sisters to argue, I worried that it added to Mom's anxiety. She was constantly yelling at us to stop.

Helping care for my younger brothers and sister became my responsibility, and although I loved them with all my heart and had strong nurturing instincts, I really wasn't old enough to take care of them. In addition to this responsibility, I washed dishes, folded laundry, vacuumed, dusted, and scrubbed the bathrooms. For some strange reason, though, I enjoyed sucking

up all the dust bunnies from the hardwood floors with the vacuum attachment. Obsessed with perfection, I couldn't leave even one tiny speck of dust or dirt. I tried to help as much as I could, but the stress of worrying about Mom, watching over my brothers and sister, doing my homework, practicing, and reading my Sunday school lessons was overwhelming. Dad later told me that I was his "left hand" and that he would never forget the help I gave him when Mom was so sick.

During Mom's mental illness, I don't think we would have made it without the help of our pastor and church friends, especially Mr. and Mrs. Emde. Although the Emdes didn't have much money, they prepared many delicious meals for us. Other friends from the church also brought meals, and some offered to help with our laundry, no small chore for a family of eight.

When Mom's doctor suggested that a weekend away might help her, the Emdes came to stay with us. Mom had been too weak to wash the kitchen curtains, so Gloria did it while she was gone. When my parents returned from their weekend away and walked through the back door and Mom saw the freshly washed, white, starched curtains, she cried. That small act of kindness meant so much to my mom.

I only remember two birthdays. On the morning of my 12th birthday, Daddy told me to go outside because he wanted to talk to me. I thought I was in trouble for something and immediately began to panic. But when I opened the back door to go outside, there, on the sidewalk, was a beautiful, new, pink and silver Schwinn bike. It even had streamers and a horn, and the chrome was so shiny I could see myself in it. How in the world, I wondered, could they afford such an expensive gift? My excitement was marred only by my suspicions that Dad was trying to buy my silence, but it still made me feel important and loved. When I turned "sweet 16 " and Bumpy turned 17, Mom gave us a really neat beach party at Lake Michigan's Jean Klock Park. Our family and church and school friends, including Barbara and Albert Liedtke, attended the party.

During summer vacation one year, Bumpy and I went to Milan, Michigan, to spend a week with Aunt Madeline and Uncle Horace, Mom's older sister and brother-in-law. They had a big garden in their back yard, and we helped them pick vegetables. The kitchen windowsills were always lined with not-so-ripe tomatoes. I wanted to tell Aunt Madeline what Dad was doing to me, but whenever I thought I had enough courage, the pain in my stomach would change my mind. Fear kept me from telling. When it all came out years later, Aunt Madeline's voice was incredibly sad as she said, "I only wish I had

known so I could have helped you."

I was about 12 years old at this time and had just started my periods. I was always grateful when I was on my period, because Dad wouldn't have anything to do with me when I was bleeding. Although they only lasted a couple days, I told Dad that they lasted a week. That one week out of every month was the only time I felt safe.

From talking to my girlfriends at slumber parties and school, I learned that intercourse was when a man put his penis inside a woman's vagina. This subject always seemed to make my girlfriends snicker and say, "Yuck, I don't even want to think about my parents doing that!" I wondered if any of my friend's daddies were doing the same thing to them. These conversations embarrassed me and made me feel terribly uncomfortable, even though my friends had no idea what was happening to me.

For reasons I didn't understand, Dad was forcing me to have intercourse with him more often. He must have looked at pornographic pictures before coming to my bedroom, because he always had an erection. Much later in my life, I thought that maybe the intercourse increased during this time because Mom was too ill to maintain any level of intimacy with Dad. This did not in any way, of course, justify what he did.

After Dad would abuse me, I would lie awake all night because I was afraid to close my eyes. I was plagued with fatigue and headaches caused from lack of sleep. Sometimes the headaches made me so sick that I would vomit at school.

Just before I started to attend junior high school, I finally realized that it wasn't normal for fathers to have sex with their daughters and that it was a sin. I was afraid to tell anyone though, because Dad continued to remind me that if Mom found out it would kill her. She was still very ill, so I believed him. I wasn't allowed to question him. If I did, he would slap the tar out of me. The torment in my mind continued day and night. I worried that Mom would find out, that someone would catch Dad, that one of my brothers or friends would suspect, or that I would get pregnant.

I knew I was different than my friends at church and school. My underwear always felt wet and slimy—wet from the discharge caused by the intercourse—slimy from the Vaseline. If that wasn't bad enough, my panties always had an unpleasant odor. When I looked in the mirror every morning, I saw a pitiful, unhappy, oily face. My shiny complexion was dreadful, because it made my face look dirty. To make matters worse, I had crooked, buck teeth, hand-me-down clothes, and hair on my legs. I felt ugly inside and out.

Dad was violating my innocent body and forcing me to do something that no child should ever have to do. Sometimes he used rubbers and sometimes he didn't, and I told him that I was afraid I would get pregnant. "Don't worry, I'll pull out before I come," was his clever response. He almost always used Vaseline, and Vaseline is nearly impossible to get off. I scrubbed and scrubbed and scrubbed some more, until I was almost raw, and still could not get rid of that dreadful greasy feeling.

I knew I had to do something to make Dad stop, but how—how could I make it stop? Nothing had helped so far, not even the wishes I had made with the "wish bone" or when I blew out the candles on my birthday cakes. I had to find a way. The only thing I knew to do was pray to my Father in heaven, the one I had learned about in Sunday school....

Seven

Music, Music, Music

Mom played the trumpet in an all-girls band when she was in high school, and Dad dabbled with the saxophone. It was Mom's desire especially, that each of us play a musical instrument.

Students could take band in fifth grade, and when I and each of my siblings turned ten years old or started fifth grade, whichever came first, my parents bought us a used instrument. Dad found Bumpy a used King cornet for $150. He plays that same instrument today, and the tone is still clear and beautiful. I wanted to play the French horn, but Daddy said I was too small to carry it to school, so I got a flute. My first flute was a $90.00 Bundy student model. Although I couldn't make a sound on it for several months, I was determined and soon made up for lost time. Mike played the trombone, Jeff played the clarinet, and Timmy played the cornet. Tammy wanted to be just like me, so she played the flute also. I took piano lessons too, and Jeff later learned how to play the piano as well. As soon as we were old enough, we joined the church orchestra and choir. Mom had a strong alto voice, and choir was a lot of fun because Mom and I sat next to each other in the alto section.

Daily practice was expected. If we didn't practice our instruments, we got punished. My brothers often had to be reminded, but not me. I was taking private flute lessons with John Bridgham and wanted to practice every day. He was eccentric, yet kind, and he had perfect pitch and often bought music and records for me. He would mysteriously walk around the music room with a cup of coffee in his hand, seldom looking at me directly, but, rather, gazing off into space. I didn't think he wasn't paying attention to what I was playing, but in reality, by not watching me, he was using his keen sense of hearing to detect imperfection in my intonation and sound. I loved to practice the flute and piano, especially my flute. My younger brothers would often knock on my bedroom door and ask if they could lie on my bed and listen to me practice. They're all grown up now, but they still enjoy listening to me.

The happiest times in my childhood were spent playing my flute, whether practicing or playing in school, church, or for the senior citizens. I knew God had called me to minister with my flute. My first flute offertory in church was a disaster. Bumpy and I played *He Lives*, and our pastor, Rev. Sprecher, held our book. For those who aren't musically inclined, I will endeavor to explain what happened. Cornets are Bb instruments, and flutes are C instruments. For this reason, cornet music has to be played in a different key when playing from the church hymnal, because the hymnal music is written in the key of C. Well, Bumpy didn't know how to transpose yet, so our first and only duet sounded like one big discord!

Tim Sprecher, Gary Marquardt, David Will, and the Juengling boys attended our church and all played an important part in the early development of our musicianship. David Will, long-time member of the gospel singing group The Imperials, was raised in Benton Harbor also. He was a gifted artist and played the trombone and sang. He was a couple years older and a good musician by the time we started playing our instruments. He was extremely patient while he taught us how to play by ear and endeavored to train my brothers in the technical aspects of transposing. We looked up to David, and even now, when we see him in concert occasionally, we are proud to say we know him. My good friends Henny Stiem, Diane Zwar, and Dennis Marquardt also played in the orchestra.

The Benton Harbor Junior High School had an excellent music program, and when I started junior high as a seventh grader I signed up for band. By this time, Bumpy had already been in the band for a year. In preparation for football season, marching rehearsals started in August. My first experience in a big marching band had some disappointment and surprises. One of the surprises is that I found out that I was a good marcher and that it came naturally to me. Another surprise is that I became quite popular and made new friends. This is where I met Kathy Wold, who became my best friend. She played the French horn. Kathy was always positive, and her self-confidence soon began to rub off on me and I began to feel better about myself. The disappointment came when the band director told me I had to play bells in the marching band instead of the flute. I hated carrying those bells—they were so heavy that they left dents in my already smaller-than-normal shoulders. It was a relief when I finally got to play the piccolo in ninth grade.

When football season was over and concert band started, I was back to playing my flute but disappointed that I had to play second part. By eighth grade though, I quickly moved up in the flute section, eventually taking first

chair. I was always challenged by my adversaries and motivated by the competition. While I knew it was acceptable to be competitive, I also knew I didn't always have the humble attitude God wanted me to have. Being confident was one thing, but being cocky, as was sometimes the case, was not pleasing to God. I am sure I made many enemies along the way, but at that time it didn't seem important. Getting a Number I rating at Solo and Ensemble competitions was a must. I could not and would not settle for a less-than-perfect score. Dad constantly told us to shut up and that we would never amount to anything, and this made success even more important.

Bumpy, Mike, and I were in the junior high school concert and marching bands at the same time. My brothers were good musicians also, and I thought they looked handsome in the red and black uniforms. Our band received Number I ratings every year at the concert and marching band competitions in Michigan, and I was proud to be a member.

Attending Campus Crusade for Christ and participating in Bible quizzing was exciting also. Sitting on the edge of the electronic pads waiting to leap off the chair the second we knew the answer to the question empowered me with boldness and courage. I studied the scriptures and questions for hours and was one of the best quizzers on our church team.

Eight

Bloody Beatings

Dad was a great artist, and I used to sit for hours watching him do sign painting on cars and trucks. He had a steady hand and a flair for color and style. In my opinion, he was a "master" sign painter. No matter how far the distance, I always recognized his artwork.

Dad had several unsuccessful business ventures—his lack of responsibility in the areas of judgment and finances never won him any entrepreneurial awards. He sold Christmas trees one winter on our front lawn and lost a lot of money, forcing us to take the ugliest tree off the lot. It was a straggly, silver, artificial tree. He used reverse psychology by telling us that the ugly little tree needed a home. We always felt sorry for the less fortunate, so it worked.

Every summer from the time we were in grade school, Mom often packed big lunches and took us all to Lake Michigan's Jean Klock Park to swim. Mike watched as we loaded coolers, towels, and beach balls into the car, knowing that he probably wouldn't get to go along. He wanted to go, but he just couldn't let Dad down, especially when Dad would say, "You're not going to go to the beach and let your ol' Dad down are you?" Dad thrived on putting guilt trips on all of us, especially Mike. Mike used to sit for hours on the back porch with his tackle box and fishing rod waiting for Dad to take him fishing, but Dad never showed up. It was a pathetic picture. Dad only needed Mike when there was a job to be done.

There was a time when my brothers, especially Mike, worked alongside Dad and other grown men at a local factory. Mike must have been quite young, because a special permit had to be signed to allow him to work there. Early on Saturday mornings when it was still dark and quiet and most children were still sleeping, Dad would shake Mike and tell him it was time to wake up and go to work.

Mike, about 15 years old, worked as hard as all of the men one summer,

but Dad didn't pay him. There was some story about Dad losing money and not being able to afford to pay. He promised Mike that he would buy him a new car as soon as he made the money back, but he didn't keep his promise.

The drinking, sexual abuse, and beatings didn't let up. My brothers were punished for things they didn't do or for small, insignificant pranks that most fathers overlooked. "But Dad," they pleaded. "Don't 'but' me," he'd yell back. He never allowed them to explain.

I can still hear the crack of that belt as Dad yanked it out of his belt loops. During these beatings, he would hold onto my brothers' skinny little arms so that they couldn't move, so tightly that sometimes they thought their arms would break. His favorite lines: "Stand still, or I'll break your arm!" and, "Son, this is going to hurt me more than it hurts you!" Often, after Jeff and Tim got whipped, they would go to their room and compare welts. The one who had the most blood oozing from their welts had to give the other one of their matchbox cars as a consolation prize.

The movie star Sinbad grew up in our neighborhood. He mentioned once that he used to hear the boys screaming when their Daddy whipped 'em.

One time I deceptively arranged to walk six blocks to visit a guy that I liked in junior high school. His name was John, just like my dad's. I told Mom I was going to a youth group meeting and told Kathy too. Well, wouldn't you know it, Mom, who had eyes in the back of her head, called Kathy's house and asked to speak with me. I wasn't there, and Kathy had no recourse but to tell her the truth. Dad took my telephone privileges away for a month— a terrible thing for a teenager. But the punishment I got paled in comparison to the guilt I felt from asking my best friend to lie for me.

Daddy never whipped me with the belt—he grounded me or took my telephone privileges away. Back then, I never questioned why Dad didn't beat me with his belt. But now I know. He was afraid that if he provoked me, my anger might push me into telling someone about the secret. He couldn't have taken that chance....

If this is how Dad shows his love, why do I feel so ashamed and lonely?
Who can I tell?
Who can I go to?
Who will listen?
Who will believe me?
Is there anyone who can help me?
Dad is trying to hide. I desperately want to be found....

Ten

Pregnant with Dad's Baby

In an effort to help Mom recuperate, her doctor suggested that she get a part-time job, so she started working at Beiderbeck's Bakery. She worked there every morning from 6:00 to 10:00. I was excited, because I knew Mom would bring day-old bakery goods home.

Mom and Dad's good friends, Alice and George Piner, lived down Britain Avenue a few blocks. These are the friends that often parked their car in the back yard at 522 Pipestone and sat with Mom until one of us came home from school. They did this because Mom, so tormented by her mental illness, was afraid to be left alone in the big house. They knew she wanted to take her own life.

During the summer of 1964, Dad's lies almost caught up with him. I was 13 years old. My monthly period, always every 28 days, was late. As each day passed with no sign of my period, I became more and more nervous and more and more obsessed with wiping. I began going into the bathroom constantly, at home and at school. Perhaps if I wipe a little deeper, I'll see just one drop of blood, I thought. Fear began to consume me.

Once in a while I would spend the night with Alice and George, and one morning I walked home from their house. When I got home and saw that Mom was still at work, I knew it was my chance to tell Dad that my period was two weeks late. I was so scared that I was shaking! "Dad, I think I might be pregnant. It must have happened when you didn't use a rubber," I said in a trembling, barely audible voice. "How in the world could you let this happen?" he exploded. "We'll make up a story and say that you were raped on your way home today, but we'll wait another week to see if you start your period," he said. Like a mannequin, I stood in complete silence without moving. Dad showed no concern for me, his little girl, a frightened child, and certainly no distress for Mom who was still struggling to pull herself out of a deep pit. All he could think about was saving his own neck. He made me

drink hot lemonade, telling me that it sometimes made a woman's period start.

At this same time, while Mom was still desperately trying to get well, her sister Brownie died from breast and lymph node cancer at age 43. Losing both her mother and sister in five years was a terrible blow. And yet, she made a valiant attempt to be strong.

If I'm pregnant, I thought, Mom might kill herself. And if I kill myself, she will still take her own life. So many questions—questions I couldn't possibly answer. Please God, help me start my period so that Mom won't have to suffer.

Several more days went by, and still I didn't start my period. I cried myself to sleep night after night and had nightmares about what would happen to me. Will they send me away? Will I have to go to school while I'm pregnant? Who will help take care of my brothers and sister? I was scared to death that when we told Mom it would kill her, and the fear of knowing that she would inevitably have to find out crippled me emotionally. I stayed in a constant state of anxiety and hopelessness. The only way I can describe the fear is by comparing it to a vice grip. Each day, as I waited for my period to start, the vice squeezed tighter and tighter around my chest until the pressure was so great I could barely breathe. I was in severe pain for several weeks, because I could not go number two—my physical body was simply shutting down.

And then, Dad told me that it was time to fabricate our story. Mom was working that morning, and when she returned he would tell her that *we* had something to say. Although I have not been able to remember most of that excruciating day, Mom does. She even remembers that the white shorts I was wearing that day had grass stains on the back. She said that Dad told her I was raped while walking home from Alice's and that I thought I was pregnant. Mom's reaction was immediate alarm, then disbelief, and finally, shock. She sat motionless, staring straight ahead. Her eyes were glassy, as if she were drugged. She couldn't believe what she was hearing. How in the world could this happen? she thought.

I don't know how we kept Mom from suspecting, because she could always tell when we were lying just by looking at us. I think I was so afraid that I instantly became a professional actress. Dad was accustomed to lying, so it took no effort on his part.

Mom somehow managed to pull herself together long enough to call our minister. He came over right away and talked to the three of us for a long time. He told my parents that if he could be really sure that I had been raped,

he would send me away to South Dakota to a home for unwed mothers. For some reason, he must have had some doubt. Many years later during the events of Dad's arrest and prosecution, Mom told me that she thought our minister suspected that Dad was the one who had raped me.

When I finally started my period and knew I wasn't pregnant, I sobbed uncontrollably until I literally gasped for air. Weeks of fear, worry, and stress had taken their toll. Eventually, I fell into a deep sleep. When I woke up, I had a violent bowel movement and bled from my rectum. Now I was bleeding from both ends, but I didn't care because I was so relieved that I wasn't pregnant.

After I started my period, the occurrences of intercourse lessened but didn't stop completely. When I was around Dad fully clothed, I still felt naked. When he looked at me, I knew he was fantasizing and lusting. When he hugged me, he always pressed tightly against my breasts with his chest.

The verbal abuse continued and seemed to be worse than ever. Daily, Dad continued to yell out his favorite lines to humiliate and demean us: "You dumb stupid clown." "What do I have to do, write you a book?" "You'll never amount to anything!"

Mom, on the other hand, always made an effort to uplift and encourage us. Her golden rule: "If you can't say something nice about someone, don't say anything at all." Sometimes her comments were almost humorous. One time during a family conversation about an overweight, unattractive acquaintance she said, "Oh, but she has such beautiful skin, and she is the most caring person." Mom still abides by this rule, and I have seldom heard her say anything unkind about anyone. I admire her for this endearing, Godly quality.

Dad did teach us good work ethics, and Mom instilled in us the importance of doing everything as unto the Lord. All of my siblings and I were conscientious, hard workers. No matter what we did, and no matter how humble, we did it to the best of our ability. Sloppy performance was unacceptable, failure never an option.

Eleven

More Memories

Mom spent hours canning and freezing jams, fruits, and vegetables, and I had to spend hours right alongside her. I didn't do it out of the goodness of my heart, and I complained constantly. My hands ached after hours of scrubbing cucumbers and peeling the skin off hundreds of peaches and tomatoes. But when we got to eat all those delicious canned goods, especially the dill pickles and peaches, I knew the labor had been worth it. There was absolutely nothing better than ice-cold peaches.

I made spending money by writing my brothers' book reports (I hope their teachers don't read this), cleaning Bumpy's bedroom, and baby-sitting. Bumpy's room wasn't dirty, just messy, with usually a week's worth of clothing stacked on his rocking chair. Unlike me, obsessed with neatness and organization, he never hung anything up after wearing it. I'm not sure if I cleaned his room for the measly money or because I knew Dad would punish him if he found his room in such disarray. I also baby-sat my three cousins for Aunt Karen and Uncle Kenny. I loved spending time at their apartment for several reasons, one because they always had my favorite Kraft cheese spreads in the little glass jars, and two because I thought Uncle Kenny was the most handsome man in the world. In fact, I was very jealous when he married Aunt Karen.

I had several other jobs while in high school. I had excellent penmanship, and Mrs. Butzbaugh, a wealthy lady who lived in a mansion on Old US31 in St. Joseph, hired me to write her social invitations. Her exquisite stationery was engraved with her initials, and I wrote every word with the utmost care. Sometimes Mom drove me to their home, and sometimes I went in a cab. The Butzbaugh family employed several black maids and servants, and since I had never known a family like this, it was all quite exciting. The maids prepared Mr. and Mrs. Butzbaugh's lunch, set it up on the long, cherry dining room table, and then returned to the back kitchen quarters to eat their own

meal. Mr. and Mrs. Butzbaugh always invited me to dine with them, but I felt uncomfortable and conspicuous eating at a table made for a dozen guests. I eventually summoned the courage to ask if they would mind if I ate my lunch with their servants, and they said it was fine. From that time on, I joined the gardener, the cook, and the other servants at the big butcher block.

Our neighbors, Mr. and Mrs. Parks, owned an apartment building on Britain Avenue about six blocks from our house. For several years, I washed and waxed three flights of stairs in that building. It was dark in the basement where the cleaning supplies were stored, and I was scared, so I took Tammy along for reinforcement. Even though she was seven years younger than I, she was good company and an adequate little worker.

When I got my check from Mrs. Parks every month, Tammy and I would dress up in our nicest clothes and shoes and walk downtown. Our first two stops were the dime store with the wooden floor and the library. Then we'd go to the fabric shop and pick out material. From there, we'd go to the JC Penney department store—we loved to ride on the elevators which were operated by kind, black gentlemen who wore crisply pressed uniforms and white gloves. On the way home, we always stopped at the Four Winds hamburger shop to get hamburgs and fries.

Henrietta, or Henny as I called her, was one of my best friends, our families went to the same church, and she played the accordion and piano in the orchestra. Her family spoke German most of the time, and she taught me a few words. "Dina nasa is too grose, Mrs. Stiem," I proudly proclaimed one day. As you can imagine, Henny got in trouble for teaching me to say your nose is too big. We laughed about this for a long time though, and her parents saw the humor in it also. I picked strawberries every summer with Henny on her family's farm. It wasn't fun getting up every morning at 5:30, but we had to be ready to pick by 6:00 so that we could finish before it got too hot. On my first day of picking I didn't cover my head and went home with gigantic water blisters on both ears—that day I learned the important lesson of wearing a bandana. The benefits were great—I got paid good wages, ate my weight in fresh strawberries, got to spend time with my good friend, and, most of all, got to eat Mrs. Stiem's yummy German kuchen. They were always so nice to me, and I felt at home with their family. I spent many Sunday afternoons with them, enjoying scrumptious homemade meals and cozy feather bed naps.

Mike had a paper route, and the vision of my little brother carrying that heavy bag of newspapers over his shoulder through wind, rain, sleet, and snow is still vivid. I think the bag of papers weighed as much as he did. I

went with him often when he delivered his papers, because he got lonely during his paper route and because he bought me an apple fritter from Biederbeck's bakery every time I went with him. I would do just about anything for an apple fritter. Mike put every penny he earned into his savings account, and sometimes he would go to the bank and deposit 50 cents. The tellers never made fun of him, and although it seemed a little silly to me at the time, his bank balance grew quickly.

Dad's vicious temper prevailed in our home. Sometimes he would do things that would scare us to death. When Bumpy was about 14 years old, Dad got mad at him for something. In an effort to get away from Dad, Bumpy ran out of the house. But Dad was hot on his heels, running after Bumpy and literally tackling him to the ground. Bumpy only weighed about 110 pounds at that time, and Mom was worried sick that Dad would kill him.

Another horrible memory of Dad's uncontrollable anger is when he kicked our two little six-week-old puppies up against the wall. He had his heavy wingtip shoes on, and he kicked them so hard that they went limp upon impact and died instantly. It was unbelievable, just unbelievable. Fear gripped us after seeing what Dad did to the puppies, and from that time on we did everything we could to avoid any type of conflict or confrontation with him.

On Wednesdays and Sundays, however, he put on his Christian demeanor and played the part of the doting husband and father who deeply loved God. It was during these times that I think I hated him the most.

From my bedroom on 522 Pipestone, I had a great view of our next-door neighbors. The youngest son, Dick, was several years older than I and very handsome—he looked like the actor Robert Wagner. His walk-in closet window faced my bedroom window, and I used to sit on my bed for hours and watch him get ready for his dates. He always had expensive automobiles and lots of girlfriends. I fantasized about kissing him for hours at a time and knew I had to do something to get his attention. So, I made a pair of black, flowered hip hugger bell-bottoms, the style with the below-the-belly-button waistline. In hopes that he might see me, I put my cool hip huggers on, roller-skated around the block, and purposefully stopped to retie my skates on the cement stump in front of his house. He did come out to play basketball, but, to my disappointment, never even looked my way. My brothers took advantage of my unsuccessful plan and teased me unmercifully.

Turning 15 was eventful, because I would soon be going to high school. By this time, most of my friends were plucking their eyebrows, shaving their legs, and wearing nylons. I was intrigued with eyebrow plucking, and

whenever I spent the night with my friend Diane, I watched her pluck her eyebrows. It seemed like such a grown-up thing to do. Mom didn't let me pluck my eyebrows and I didn't know how to use tweezers, so I took her razor and trimmed them. Strategically shaping my eyebrows with a clumsy razor was a little tricky, but I did it and did a pretty decent job. It's a miracle that I didn't cut myself though. Mom also said I was too young to shave my legs and that once I started, the hair would grow back darker and thicker. Being the only teenager in the world, or at least in my circle of friends, with hair on my legs and still wearing white anklets was almost scandalous. It was a day to remember when I finally got my first pair of suntan-colored nylon stockings and garter belt.

The Benton Harbor High School bands were recognized and known for their superior performances all over the state of Michigan, and my siblings and I were elated to be members. I held first chair in the flute section throughout most of high school, occasionally being challenged by another flutist. I was section leader of the piccolo squad and won the best marcher award in my senior year. Although only 100 pounds and five feet tall, I made an unforgettable impression on the marching field.

I loved the football games, running onto the field for the pre-game routines, and perfecting the kaleidoscope formations during the half-time shows. The fresh apples and clear, crisp fall weather added to the exhilaration. I didn't like memorizing the music, but I did it nonetheless. The Blossom Parade, which took place annually in May when the apple blossoms were in full bloom, was another thrilling event. I was ecstatic as I strutted down the main streets of St. Joseph and Benton Harbor in my fancy uniform, especially when someone in the crowd spotted me and excitedly screamed out, "Hey, Jody!"

Rehearsals were always right after school, and on the way home I'd always stop by Old's Dairy, the same dairy where my mom worked when she was a teenager. Mom always had lots of change in her wallet, and I raided it nearly every day. She never missed a penny, and I never missed a snack on the way home!

The orange, black, and white band uniforms, which had an extremely professional appearance, included capes, spats, and hats with plumes. If you marched correctly with your shoulders swaying, the capes created an exciting, flashy effect. Our marching director, Monte Sheedlow, fashioned our marching style after the Michigan State Marching Band with knees raised to our waists. Rehearsals were such a workout that band members were exempt from

physical education classes.

My brothers and I often stopped by my best friend's house in the morning on the way to school so that one of them could carry her heavy French horn for her. They were such gentlemen. Kathy was always, always late, and every day, just as she came running out the front door, her mom would holler, "Did you drink your instant breakfast?"

Kathy was a faithful friend and stuck by me no matter what. When I didn't have lunch money, she gave me some. She was an excellent seamstress, and when I didn't have just the right outfit to wear, she helped me sew something new or loaned me something from her own closet. I knew how to sew also but wasn't as proficient as Kathy.

When Tim and Tam became old enough to play instruments, our family became known as the family with the most children in the Benton Harbor music program. The director, Bernie Kuschel, was also our friend, and we knew that he was proud of our accomplishments. His affirmation was crucial at this time in our lives. He and his wife attended every graduation and several family weddings. Following is part of the article about the Enders Family that was featured in *The Herald-Palladium* dated June 10, 1976:

Tammy Enders is Last of Tiger Band Tradition

The graduation from Benton Harbor high school this month of Tammy Enders, 17, put the final notch in a school music record: Six children from the same family playing a total of 11 consecutive years in the Tiger marching and symphony bands. The record ends appropriately with the retirement of Bernhardt M. Kuschel, director of music programs for the school district, who has taught and directed Enders children for 17 of his 37-year career.

Tammy is the daughter and youngest child of Mr. and Mrs. John Enders, 4092 East Britain Avenue, Benton Township. Mrs. Enders said it began in 1960 when her oldest son, John, took cornet lessons in a class taught by Kuschel. John played with the high school bands from 1965-68. Joining the bands were daughter Jody, 1966-69; and sons Mike, 1967-70; Jeff, 1970-73; Tim, 1974-75; and finally, Tammy, 1973-76.

"It's a record as far as I can remember," Kuschel said Sunday. He was among some 30 family members and friends at the Enders' home for an outdoor dinner-party to salute Tammy's graduation. Kuschel

said he recalls another family with three members in his bands, but six from one family is the most in his long career.

Last year, Bumpy, Mike, Jeff, Tam, and I visited Mr. and Mrs. Kuschel at the senior home where they reside. Revisiting old times was terrific, and Mr. Kuschel, especially, had not changed at all. He still had that distinctive sense of humor. And I learned, for the first time, that Mike was accepted into the high school band even though he didn't pass the audition, only because Mr. Kuschel felt sorry for him. Mr. Kuschel used wisdom when he made that decision, perhaps more than he realized. And Mike turned out to be a good trombone player. As we said our farewells, we gathered in the sitting room and sang a couple songs from years gone by, with a promise that we would bring our instruments the next time we came to visit. Unfortunately, Mr. Kuschel passed away shortly after our visit.

The musical instruments were a financial sacrifice for my parents, but they felt it was worth it. I know it was. The wonderful memories of band will forever remain in my heart.

We weren't allowed to wear slacks in high school, so during the cold winter months my friends and I usually wore wool kilts, sweaters, and knee socks. I was ecstatic when I opened one of my Christmas gifts one year and found a beautiful Pendleton wool, black watch plaid kilt and a navy blue sweater. Mom gave $15 for the kilt, a high price in the 60s. The style then was to wear skirts above the knees, but because I wasn't allowed to wear short skirts I had to roll the waistband up several times after I got to school. No one could tell, because my sweaters covered the waistband. It felt good to get away with something!

As with many teenagers, I fell in love during high school. My first and only serious boyfriend, Jeff, was over six feet tall. He was one of the nicest guys in the high school, and I really thought I was in love with him. When he asked me to go steady and gave me his class ring, I thought I would just die. I quickly went out and bought different colors of angora thread to coordinate with my clothes and to adjust his ring to fit my size 3-1/2 finger. It was so exciting I could hardly stand it. And, as always, Kathy was there to help me compose the perfect love letters.

Our church frowned on movie theaters, so my parents didn't let me go. This too was embarrassing, because my friends often went on the weekends. When I went to see *Bonnie and Clyde* with Jeff, I had to lie to my parents and say I was going somewhere else. I was confident that Mom and Dad wouldn't

find out, but I was wrong. Our dentist drove by in his car, saw me standing in line, and reported his findings to Dad. I didn't like our dentist and always felt uncomfortable around him but never knew why. Now I really didn't like him. Dad was furious and grounded me for an entire month. I will admit that it wasn't a very wholesome movie, but being grounded for that length of time seemed extreme.

Because of Dad's strictness and the fact that our church also disapproved of dancing, I wasn't allowed to go to dances either. But in my senior year, I somehow managed to sneak to the homecoming dance with Jeff by telling my parents that it was a Homecoming party. A party is different than a dance. The DJ played *You Are My Special Angel*, our favorite love song, and we had a wonderful time. I was relieved when I returned home that evening, on time of course, and found Mom and Dad already in bed. As always, because I knew it was expected, I stepped into their bedroom and nonchalantly announced that I was home. Several months later when the school yearbooks were published and my parents came across a picture of us dancing together, Dad exploded. He grounded me for a month, another punishment that didn't fit the crime. It humiliated me, because it was such an innocent event and so much fun. The picture did look funny though with a five-foot-one-inch girl dancing with a six-foot-four-inch guy—my head came just over his waistline. Jeff, of course, couldn't possibly understand why someone would be grounded for going to a chaperoned school dance. He wanted to go to the senior prom and knew he couldn't take me, so he asked one of my friends. I wasn't mad at him, just very, very hurt. I never thought I would get over it, and many years went by before I was able to forgive Dad.

Dad was way too hard on all of us. He didn't use love or wisdom when he disciplined us, and because of his ludicrous harshness I missed out on a lot. I could never understand how he could be such a strict disciplinarian while his own life was full of sin. I hated him for it.

Twelve

Moving Next Door

It was about this time that my parents decided to move next door to 542 Pipestone Road. It was a bigger house and considerably nicer, yet still affordable at $200 a month. After Dad refinished all of the hard wood floors and winding staircase, it looked like something out of a movie. From the second story, you could look down over the staircase railing and see the front door and entryway. I dreamed of someday floating gracefully down that incredible staircase in a long, flowing elegant gown. It never happened.

The kitchen was quite small, because the sole purpose for this room at the time the house was built was for food preparation. It also had a back staircase for the maids that used to be employed. The huge dining room and living rooms featured oak fireplaces with carved lion heads, glass-front bookshelves, and floor-to-ceiling sliding oak doors. The massive front door was oak and glass and had an interesting brass knocker that was probably a family insignia many years earlier. Other rooms included an entryway with a stained glass window (which Mike now has in his home), a poolroom, five bedrooms, two bathrooms, and a porch that Mom and Dad turned into a bedroom for themselves.

It was so cold in their bedroom that we seldom went in there, and I wondered how Mom managed to stay warm. One time there was a leak in the roof over their bedroom. When Mom crawled in bed that night and she felt the ice cold, wet sheets on Dad's side of the bed, she quickly moved to her side. When he finally came to bed and the shock of the ice cold, wet sheets hit his skin, he jumped out of bed! And then Mom broke out into spontaneous laughter. I could hardly believe that she had the nerve to go through with such a prank. Even more unbelievable was the fact that Dad didn't get mad.

Mike had the octagon-shaped bedroom at the top of the stairs to the left. For some reason, Dad used Mike's room when he whipped the boys with his belt. He kept his room neat and organized at all times. Mom made plaid

curtains, and I made a baseball caddie from striped denim for storing his baseball, glove, and bat. It was a difficult sewing project, and I was very proud when it was finished. It was nice to give him something I had made all by myself.

Tammy and I shared a bedroom across the hall from Mike's. Mom bought twin beds and matching pale turquoise and white chenille bedspreads from a church friend. After she added lavender throw rugs and delicate white curtains with lavender trim, our room looked quite feminine. The mirror and miniature sink in the small closet that adjoined our room to Tim and Jeff's bedroom was a novelty. I had acne and used to pop my zits every morning in front of that mirror. Other than the dirty mirror, everything was impeccably organized and neat in our room, so neat, in fact, that I always knew when one of my brothers had trespassed.

This is the bedroom where Tammy once played a cruel trick on me. When I returned home late from a date one night, I tiptoed quietly up the stairs to my room so I wouldn't wake anyone. She had been waiting under my bed for me, and just as I started to climb into bed, a hand reached out and grabbed my ankle. I think that's the only time I was ever really furious with my little sister.

Tim and Jeff shared a bedroom next to ours. Tim's bed was always neat, because I taught him how to make it. Bumpy had his own room next to theirs. He was a slob and never made his bed.

Every spring, the ground at 542 Pipestone blossomed with thick clusters of Lily of the Valley. I had a first-rate view of these delicately shaped miniature bells from my bedroom, and when I opened a window, the sweet fragrance of the tiny blooms immediately filled my senses. I picked many bouquets for Mom and myself.

Both homes were beautiful, and I never understood why they were destroyed years later. The plans to build a children's home on that property never developed. Fortunately, Mike was able to get some of the globe lamps and a stained glass window before the homes disappeared. Even though the physical structures are gone, I will never forget what they looked like. Sometimes I want to forget, but I can't. When my daughter drove me around my old neighborhood recently and we turned into what used to be the driveway of 522 Pipestone Road, only the big evergreen and the lilac bushes remained. And yet, in my heart and memories, the house was still there....

Thirteen

A Near-Tragic Boating Accident

Dad did not rape me after we moved. He tried to talk me into it one time, but I was older and wiser. With a boldness and determination unknown to me, my voice shattered the silence like an echo in a mountain valley as I coldly stated, "No Dad, not anymore. Don't ever touch me again or I'll tell!" I believe that the words that came out of my mouth were from the voice of authority, that of my Heavenly Father, warning Dad to never harm me again. It was an indescribable victory!

Shortly after this, my brother Mike almost lost his life because of Dad's drinking. Here is that story, with some portions taken directly from *The News Palladium*[1] article dated Monday, April 1, 1968:

At the end of March in 1968, my dad, his brother Stub, and a friend decided to take their 15-foot runabout out into icy Lake Michigan in preparation for the upcoming Coho fishing season. Mike was nearly always by Dad's side, so he was invited to go along. And, as usual, Dad and Uncle Stub had been drinking.

It was late afternoon as they headed out into the lake. About four miles out, the gas line ruptured. Dad and Uncle Stub tried to fix it, but in the commotion, the boat took on water. This, combined with the stiff breeze, which was common at that time of year on Lake Michigan, caused the boat to dip, fill with water, and overturn.

They were all wearing lifejackets. It was almost dusk. After remaining with the boat for several minutes, all four decided to split up with Dad and Mike heading for shore. Dad later admitted that he thought they were all going to drown. Mike said he was scared to death, and he was almost certain he was going to die. While he was in that icy water, he thought about all of his personal belongings and what he would want each of his brothers and sisters to have if he died. He wanted me to have his oxford button-down collar shirts.

Meanwhile, Mr. Bergum was parked alongside the north pier and was chatting with a friend when an unidentified youngster came running up and said that people fishing on the pier thought they saw a boat out in the lake earlier but could not see it now. Bergum recalled seeing a boat earlier also, and he decided to investigate.

He immediately headed west into the lake, and shortly afterwards, spotted dots on the water. His wife was at the wheel of their boat, *Fair Weather Love*, and Bergum was on the bow. The rescue began.

The first one aboard was Mike, then Dad, followed by Uncle Stub and then their friend. They were in the water approximately 30 minutes and would not have lasted another 15 minutes. They were so weak they had to be dragged into the Bergum's boat, and they looked like lobsters. At the coast guard station, they were all thawed out in hot showers. According to the Coast Guard, it was a tragedy narrowly averted!

I clearly remember every detail of that night. Mom had just finished washing her hair when the telephone rang. "Barb, bring some dry clothes to the Coast Guard for me and Mike," Dad yelled.

"What do you mean, bring some dry clothes? What in the world happened?"

"We've been swimming in the lake for 30 minutes, that's what happened!" he yelled in an ugly, harsh tone of voice. We could hardly believe what we were hearing!

Mom and I quickly gathered some clothes and headed for the Coast Guard. When we arrived, then, and only then, did Mom realize that Mike had almost lost his life because of Dad's drinking and irresponsibility. When we got back home, Dad left almost immediately to go to the Parkmore, a local bar, saying his brother needed him. Once again, no concern for his family.

Mike still suffers from dreadful pain in his limbs caused by the effects of being in the ice-cold water for so long.

Nothing was mentioned in the newspaper article about Dad being drunk. If he hadn't been drinking, this accident probably wouldn't have happened. Maybe the ice cold water sobered him up before he was picked up by the Coast Guard. We will never know.

Fourteen

My First Kiss

During my adolescent and early teen years, I attended camp in Bridgman, Michigan, every summer with friends from my church and other Assembly of God churches all over the state and Canada. Packing for camp was so exciting that I'd start sorting everything on my bedroom floor several months in advance. I needed casual outfits, church outfits, sheets and blankets, swimsuit, towels, toiletries, and snacks. We weren't allowed to wear slacks, so our casual outfits consisted of dresses or skirts and blouses.

Our dentist's wife (married to the same dentist that tattled on me) gave me hand-me-down clothes, mostly shirtwaist dresses. I liked the dresses, but it was embarrassing when Maryjane came up to me in front of my friends at camp and said, "Oh, I remember that old dress!" She wasn't being unkind, because she was a nice girl; she just didn't understand that her words hurt my feelings.

Two girls shared one room, and every day after the counselors inspected each room, the "cleanest room award" was announced. I took pride in the fact that my room won often, although I grew impatient with my sloppy roommates who had to be constantly and firmly reminded to keep their side tidy. We looked forward to playing tricks on our counselors. One year, we managed to get into some of their rooms and put baby powder under their bed sheets. When several of the male counselors got up from their afternoon naps, there were a variety of responses when they realized that their black dress trousers were covered with white baby powder. They were good sports though and laughed right along with us. The pop stand opened daily for several hours before and after the evening services. To those who could afford it, a variety of ice cream, soft drinks, potato chips, and candy bars were available. Spending money wasn't a luxury, so I felt fortunate if one of the guys bought me a treat. The pop stand was the camp hang out, especially in the evenings. That's where most of the kids did their serious flirting!

I had a crush on an older guy named Dan, and one summer he invited me to go to the banquet with him. This special dress-up event was held at the end of camp week, and the guys wore suits and the girls wore fancy dresses. I could hardly believe it. I was going to the banquet with Dan. It wasn't really a date—we just walked into the decorated cafeteria together and sat next to each other during dinner. On the last day of camp, while leaning against a giant, friendly oak, Dan kissed me. I thought I would faint from the excitement even though his mother was watching.

In 1968, our church youth group went to Detroit over the Memorial Day weekend to attend a big youth retreat. Although Dan and I had not kept in contact on a consistent basis, I was excited about seeing him again. In anticipation, I bought a new sea foam colored polka dot dress and MaryJane shoes to match. We sat together and held hands during every church service. He took me to his parents' apartment one afternoon, and we sat on the living room couch and kissed for an hour. The desire to have sex with him right then and there was overwhelming! At the end of the rally, I waved good-bye to Dan from my seat on the church bus as it pulled away from the parking lot, hoping to see him again soon.

That same summer, I spent a week with Aunt Ellie and Uncle Tanke in Huntington Woods, not far from Sterling Heights where Dan and his family lived. Aunt Ellie was a cool aunt, and she liked Dan, so she let me go to the Detroit Zoo with him. I wore tan slacks and a pale pink button-down collar oxford shirt that I had borrowed from my brother Mike. I felt grown up and special riding in Dan's new, expensive car. I was invited to have dinner with him and his parents one evening and was overwhelmingly intimidated. They were very financially stable and had a lovely home with wall-to-wall orange carpet, something I thought was spectacular. I had never used two spoons and two forks before and didn't know which piece of silver to use first. His parents seemed surprised that I didn't know what to do. I sensed that they didn't think I was good enough for their son.

Once again, thoughts of failure and unworthiness crept into my mind...

Fifteen

Getting Engaged and Escaping to College

During my senior year of high school, I participated in the Southwestern Michigan Junior Miss Contest. I wasn't optimistic about winning, but I thought it would be fun and looked forward to the talent portion of the competition.

Mom and I sat down to calculate what I would need for each phase of the contest and how much it would cost. Let's see: a tailored, conservative outfit for the judge's interview, a semi-formal dress for the talent contest, a full-length evening gown, and of course shoes to coordinate with every outfit. How would we ever squeeze enough money out of an already sparse budget for all these new clothes? Mom had become a master at robbing Peter to pay Paul as she used to say, so I had no doubt she could pull it off.

I sewed a vest and skirt out of green wool tweed for the judge's interview. An inexpensive pale yellow blouse completed the ensemble. To our delight, we discovered a beautiful ivory-colored polyester, street-length chemise with a pleated bodice for the talent portion. For the evening gown event, we found a simple, elegant pale pink dress that featured a fabric rose on the bodice.

I'm sure I didn't score very high in the judge's interview, because I was terrified to speak by myself in front of a group. I did do well in the talent and evening gown segments though. In my floor-length pale pink evening gown I felt like I was beautiful, perhaps for the first time in my life. And I confidently walked out onto the platform in front of all those people and performed a difficult classical piece by memory entitled "Concertino" by Chaminade. When the last note was played and I removed my flute from my lips, my flute teacher (also the high school Latin teacher), John Bridgham, stood and began to applaud. Soon everyone in the audience was standing. At that moment, as I took my bow, the Jr. Miss crown no longer mattered. The entire week was a lot of fun and instilled in me the desire to achieve perfection in everything I did. And the sacrifices Mom made for me were very meaningful.

Also in my senior year, my brother and I entered the Assemblies of God

Christ Ambassador's Talent Contest. Reverend C. M. Ward, the well-known voice of Revivaltime Choir in Springfield, Missouri, was one of the judges. What an exciting weekend! Bumpy entered the vocal competition, singing "Same Old-Fashioned Way." I accompanied him on the piano and remember that the four sharps in the key signature made me extremely nervous. My selection for the instrumental contest was a unique, technical version of "When We All Get to Heaven," with three movements and double tonguing. I was stunned when I was awarded 1st Place Instrumental. I proudly displayed my trophy in our home for many years and only recently gave it to my niece, Kayla, who is also playing the flute. It was during this weekend, with the encouragement of Mom and Rev. Ward, along with the possibility of several scholarships, that I made the decision to go to Evangel College in Springfield, Missouri, to major in music.

When I graduated from high school, Dan surprised me with a beautiful jade necklace and earrings, my first expensive jewelry with authentic stones. His parents gave me a matching jade bracelet. After the graduation ceremony, I proudly showed off the baubles to my friends. During the summer after graduation, we fell in love and Dan gave me a simple, but exquisite diamond solitaire and asked me to marry him. I didn't think his parents approved of me, so I was pleasantly surprised when I received a congratulations card from them that stated, "We are very happy for you."

We lived three hours apart, so I eagerly looked forward to receiving mail. No matter where I was in that big house when the mailman came, I recognized the grating sound of the mailbox lid opening and closing. I don't think a day went by that I didn't get a card or letter from Dan. Throughout the summer months, he frequently drove from Sterling Heights to Benton Harbor so we could spend weekends together. My sister, about ten years old at that time, really liked the attention he bestowed on her. She monopolized his time and always wanted to sit on his lap when he came to visit, and it annoyed me. He was patient with her though, perhaps because he never had a sister.

As summer came to a close and the days became shorter, I prepared to leave for Evangel College. I was ready, or I thought I was ready, to leave my home and family. I loved Dan, but I wanted to experience college, take advantage of the scholarships, and more than anything, fulfill my dream of getting my music degree and becoming a professional flutist. Most importantly, I wanted to get away from Dad!

It was Labor Day weekend 1969, and Mom, Dad, Tammy and I drove the 15 hours to Springfield. My parents got me settled into my dorm, which was

an old Army barracks. The first dormitory was still under construction, and even if it had been finished I wouldn't have been able to afford to live there. All too soon, it was time for my family to return to Michigan and I could see tears in Mom's eyes. As I watched them drive away and realized that I was being left all alone far from home without my mom for the first time in my life, I started to cry.

During Thanksgiving break, when most students went home to be with their families, I went south on the band tour. In Biloxi, Mississippi, there was destruction everywhere from Hurricane Camille. Having never experienced the power and wrath of a hurricane, I was astounded that a 32-foot wave had the power to pick up large boats and set them on shore. It was an incredible sight. We ministered every evening at a different church, some with fewer than 100 members and some with several 1000 members.

I enjoyed my college experience, and although I never adjusted to being away from home, the break from Dad was like balm on my open wounds....

Sixteen

A Tiny New Life and Marriage

I missed my fiancé and was desperate to be with him, so I left college. He drove all the way to Missouri to get me, and on the way home, we spent the night in a hotel. I saved the menu, a chicken bone, and the shampoo label from our night together and put it in a scrapbook. Many years later when my daughter was looking at the scrapbook, I had to offer an honest explanation.

Although we didn't plan to get married right away, an unexpected pregnancy soon changed those plans. I remember the day we told my parents that I was pregnant. I was frantic, and Dan did his best to support me. This would be the second time that I had had to expose an unexpected pregnancy. Mom was terribly disappointed and hurt, of course, but she didn't get mad. As always, she reassured me that she loved me and would support me. Dad, however, became livid. I wanted to believe that his anger was justified because of his concern for my future, but I believe it was due to his jealousy that another man had been intimate with me. It was one of the worst days in my life, one I will never forget.

My parents would have never contemplated asking us to give our baby away, but Dan's parents felt we should give it up for adoption. We told them that under no circumstances would we consider giving up our child. It was not an option. We had conceived this new life together and were very much in love, and we had no intentions of giving our baby away. They were more concerned about their reputation than our baby's well being. Their advice hurt me terribly and tainted our relationship even more.

My in-laws' lifestyle caused concern and doubt for me. On Sundays, my father-in-law sang in the church choir and ushered and my mother-in-law played the organ. But on the weekends, they often went out and played cards, smoked, and drank. They were living on both sides of the fence just as my dad had done for so many years. I never said anything to them, but I did tell my mother-in-law that she could not hold my baby while she was smoking.

It's sad that the only positive thing I can say about my father-in-law is that he showed me how to fold fitted sheets, a skill I have found useful throughout my life.

We were married on February 28, 1970, in a small, informal wedding at the Assembly of God in Detroit, Michigan. It was 65 degrees that day, unseasonably warm for that time of year. Dan wore a dark blue suit, and I wore an ivory street-length dress with a headpiece designed and made by Aunt Ellie. Bumpy's fiancée, Shelly, was my maid of honor, and Dan's brother was the best man. Pastor Alvin Sprecher performed the ceremony, and Kathy attended the wedding. We received many nice gifts, including several sets of orange and avocado green flowered sheets—that color scheme makes it seem so long ago.

Dan was still in college and we had no money coming in and no savings, so Aunt Ellie and Uncle Tanke invited us to share their home with them. Knowing that we were newlyweds, they unselfishly gave us their bedroom while they slept on the lumpy roll-a-way bed in the family room downstairs. They never asked us for any money, and I never heard them complain. I always wondered why my in-laws didn't offer us a room in their big, fancy home in Sterling Heights.

Every morning, Aunt Ellie made oatmeal while I packed my lunch, a bologna sandwich and piece of fruit. I had a temporary secretarial assignment at General Motor's Headquarters in downtown Detroit and rode to work every day with Uncle Tanke and his friends. Sometimes the wind was so strong as it whipped around those big buildings that the big black guard had to help me cross the street. Saks Fifth Avenue was located on the main floor of the General Motor's building, and during my lunch I browsed through the petite section. I couldn't afford the high prices, so I drew pictures of some of the maternity dresses. The sales ladies gave me outlandish looks, but I didn't care. I purchased fabric and sewed the same dresses for a fraction of the cost.

We eventually saved enough money to rent a small, three-room basement apartment across from the zoo in Royal Oak. It was filthy when we first moved in; the stove and kitchen walls were covered with grease. But with a lot determination, hard work, and shiny white paint, we turned it into a cozy first home.

Dan went to school, and I continued to work as a secretary. I began suffering with morning sickness and threw up every day on the way. It was strange, because this almost always happened at the same intersection while the same song, "Bridge Over Troubled Water," was playing on the radio.

Aunt Ellie and Mom had a big baby shower for me. I made myself a special designer original for the occasion, one I had sketched from Saks Fifth Avenue. It was sleeveless with a ruffled neckline, made out of light blue dotted Swiss fabric. Again, my friend Kathy was there to support me. She bought me a darling set of china baby dishes. After opening all of the wonderful baby gifts, I began looking forward to being a mother. I only gained 10 pounds during the entire nine months and was told that it was a record at the hospital in Royal Oak. On the exact due date, September 30, after one hour of mild labor, our 6-1/2 pound precious daughter was born. I wanted to name her Mary Elizabeth, but my mother-in-law didn't like that name. I allowed her control and intimidation pressure me into giving my baby a different name, although I did eventually love the name Dawn Renee. My mom nicknamed her 'Lil Peeps.

The day Dawnie was born is truly one of the happiest days of my life. I felt so complete. Although I was only 19 years old, I knew I would be a good mother. Dan brought us home from the hospital in our new red Volkswagen Beetle, and when we pulled into the driveway of our apartment, Mom, Tammy, Jeff and Tim were waiting for us. Jeff was the first one to the car and was also the first one to hold Dawnie. It was love at first sight, and from that day on, Dawnie became the center of attention. She brought so much joy into my family that we wondered how we ever existed without her. Dan's family loved her also.

When she was three weeks old, against my doctor's advice, I went back to work because we needed the income. Once again, Aunt Ellie came through for us by offering to take care of Dawnie. I cried all the way to work every morning after I dropped my new baby off at Aunt Ellie's house. I was appreciative and thankful for the love and attention I knew Aunt Ellie would give our baby, but it was still very sad to leave her.

During the Viet Nam War, Dan was drafted into the United States Army. After he left for basic training, Dawnie and I moved to Benton Harbor to live with my parents in the big house on 542 Pipestone. What a great time we had! Bumpy was married, Mike was attending Trinity Bible College in North Dakota, and Jeff, Tim, and Tammy were still living at home. Every day after school, they argued over whose turn it was to take Dawnie for a stroller ride. Dad and the boys let her sit in the middle of their expensive pool table and roll the balls from one corner to the other—this entertained them more than the game.

When Dan graduated from boot camp, Kathy and I drove to Kentucky.

After graduation, Dan was sent to Monterey, California, where he served his country as a chaplain's assistant. He was very meticulous and took pride in every aspect of his responsibilities. After he got an apartment, Dawnie and I joined him. For our airplane trip, I made matching purple, polyester dresses. We enjoyed the incredible scenery and wonder of the ocean during the year we lived there. Even though we couldn't afford to purchase any furniture, we made sure our baby had a tiny artificial Christmas tree and a Christmas stocking. The tree had one string of lights and one ornament, a red plastic apple. (Now, she and her husband hang it on their tree every year.)

We were extremely concerned that Dan might get sent to Viet Nam, so when he received orders to go to Germany we were relieved. When Dawnie was about 18 months old, the two of us made the eight-hour flight on the big Lufthansa 747 to Germany. As I said good-bye to Mom and Dad at O'Hare Airport in Chicago, we all cried and Mom almost collapsed. Her grief was so severe that Dad had to help her walk out of the airport. Letting their first grandchild go, especially all the way to Germany, almost broke their hearts. Dawnie enjoyed the trip immensely, running up and down the aisles in her pink "feety" pajamas, entertaining the stewardesses and other passengers.

Although it broke my heart to leave my mom, I ached for my husband. We had a healthy, wonderful sex life, and I longed to be with him again.

Dan continued his career as a chaplain's assistant to Chaplain Zimmerman, and I helped out in the halfway house preparing meals for the soldiers. I also taught Sunday school and played my flute in some of the Sunday services. All the soldiers on the base loved Dawnie, and she took every opportunity to show off for them. We bought two bikes, and while Dan was at work during the day I put Dawnie in her baby seat and the two of us rode for hours. We could never pass a roadside stand without buying a bag of Gummi Bears for her. One by one, she would unmercifully bite the little heads off each colorful, chewy bear.

At the end of November in 1972, when I was about three months pregnant with our second child, Dawnie and I returned to Michigan. I cannot describe the look on my parents' faces when they first saw their precious 'Lil Peeps. She was sitting on one of our suitcases on the main floor of O'Hare Airport, and they were standing on the second floor looking over the balcony. When she looked up and spotted them, she pointed with her tiny pointer finger and whispered, "Poppop." Mom and Dad couldn't hear her, but they had no trouble reading her lips. During the two-hour drive from Chicago to Benton Harbor, all she could say was "fie fies, fie fies." She wanted McDonald's French

fries!

When Dan was discharged from the Army a couple months later, Dad helped him get a job in the factory at Leco Corporation where he and my brother Mike worked. We rented a darling two-bedroom house a couple blocks from the high school. We were very happy to be back in the United States with our family.

The apple blossoms were in full bloom when our son was born in May, my favorite time of year. He was short and chubby at 8-1/2 pounds and 19 inches long. We named him Matthew Aaron from the Bible. Dr. Conybeare, the same doctor who delivered all of my siblings and me, also delivered Matthew. I didn't experience any labor pain before or during the delivery. Dr. Conybeare said I was just like my mother. I didn't have to go back to work right away, so I had the wonderful experience of breast-feeding Matthew for a year—it was an extraordinary time of bonding.

No two children are alike, and I soon learned just how different my two were. Dawnie was spontaneous, loved to laugh, and got into everything. The more attention she got, the happier she was. Sometimes she was naughty just to get attention. She slept with her favorite blanket that she called maako. Although worn and tattered and without the original silk ribbon edging and animal designs, she still loves this blanket and sleeps with it every night—she even took it on her honeymoon. Matthew was serious and quiet and could entertain himself for hours as long as he had something to read and bunbun, his favorite stuffed animal. Mom and I reconstructed bunbun's eyes, nose, and mouth over and over again until it resembled anything but a bunny. Nevertheless, he loved it, and it went everywhere with us. He couldn't even go to sleep without it.

Dan and I eventually rented a bigger house in the country. Dad and Mike refinished the hardwood floors in our living room and bedrooms, Bumpy remodeled the bathroom using leftover wallpaper from his business, and Dan and I painted. The green and white gingham checked curtains I sewed provided the finishing touch to my children's bedroom. Our rent was late almost every month, and we would have been homeless had it not been for the patience and kindness of our landlord, Karl Grenawitzki. It made me sick every time I had to call him and tell him that our rent was going to be late—Dan said that telephone calls of this nature were my responsibility.

It was fun living on Napier Avenue, because Mike, Tim, and my parents all had homes within walking distance. Mom and Dad had recently moved from 542 Pipestone to the country into a big old farmhouse on Hillandale

Avenue, about one mile away.

In addition to the fresh eggs that our chickens provided each morning, we had a big garden that yielded lots of fresh vegetables. I worked many hours every week making sure our garden didn't have any weeds. As with every area in my life, my garden had to be organized. We grew corn, cucumbers, squash, green beans, radishes, carrots, and tomatoes. Our children helped by pulling weeds. Matthew played in the garden for hours, parking his little matchbox cars in between the rows of vegetables. After playing in the garden, my children looked like they belonged to Aunt Jemima instead of me. The kids sold the vegetables at a little roadside stand in the front yard and always got excited when someone stopped to buy something.

Several years after we were married while my in-laws were visiting, my father-in-law decided to help Dan clean our basement. When he came across my treasure box and found out what was in it, he sternly said, "You're married to my son now; you don't need these things any more." And with that, he promptly threw away something that was irreplaceable, a shoebox filled with priceless memories, mostly from junior and senior high school—letters that my girlfriends and I had passed back and forth in class, cards and letters from my boyfriend, solo and ensemble award ribbons, an old diary, and many photographs. He also threw my china doll away because he said it wasn't worth anything without hair. My treasure box was my private property, and no one had any right to take it away, but intimidation kept me from speaking up. I know my daughter would have enjoyed looking at the photographs and reading the letters, and who knows what I would have discovered in the diary.

Dan's parents felt that I had ruined their son's life and that I wasn't good enough for him, and maybe this was their way of getting revenge.

After Dan and I had been married for about five years, I experienced a critical and traumatic turning point in my life when Dad asked me if I wanted to go on a short, overnight trip with him in his semi. It didn't occur to me that he would try anything, because he hadn't touched me since I was about 15 years old. I looked forward to spending some time with him and hoped to have an opportunity to ask him why he had sexually molested me, something we had never discussed. But to my disappointment, shock, and disbelief, Dad propositioned me in the hotel. With a pouty lip and his head hanging down, he said, "I don't suppose you want to fool around once more for old time's sake do you?" I could not believe what I was hearing. Surely I had misunderstood. How could he possibly think that I would consider something

so immoral and outrageous!

I tried to ignore what happened, knowing that if I told Mom it would shatter her heart into a million pieces. And my children loved their poppop so much. I was torn. My head was telling me one thing. My heart was telling me something else. It was then that I realized Dad was still living to satisfy his own perverted, selfish desires with no regard for the consequences or anyone else's feelings. It seemed as though he had literally disappeared into the perverted disease that he allowed to control his mind. I believe that Dad had the power to make the right choices, but he made them in darkness. I was faced with a choice too and knew I had no alternative but to smother the repulsive thing that Dad had done and leave it deep in the most secret place of my heart.

Many years later I found out that Dad was still doing his best to mess around with Tammy. She was in high school and living at home with Mom and Dad, and one day she told Mom she wanted a lock on her bedroom door. Mom, somewhat surprised, said, "Why would you want a lock on your door? Dad and I are here with you all the time." Tammy's response was brief and straightforward. "I would just feel better if I had a lock." Tammy must have foreseen what was to come, because shortly after the lock was installed, Dad knocked on her bedroom door one night and said, "Tammy, let me in. I want to show you something. I took some kind of medicine that made my penis get really big." Again, Tammy's response was short and to the point. "No, Dad, I won't let you in."

Dan, I, and our children were faithful members of First Assembly of God in Benton Harbor. Dan served as a board member and was active in Royal Rangers. I taught Sunday school, played in the orchestra, and sang in the choir. We had many loyal, precious friends in this church. Albert Liedtke, especially, played an integral part in our lives. He was someone we admired and respected, a Godly, humble man who supported and prayed for us.

When we weren't in church, we were with my parents on their farm. It was the central meeting place for our entire family. More than anything else, our children loved spending time with Gamgam and Poppop. There was always something exciting going on at the farm: mamma kitty giving birth to a new litter of soft, cuddly balls of fluff; Uncle Tim, Aunt Marla and their horses; picking corn and fruit; hay rides; running through the sprinkler; sitting in the swing watching the sunsets; picnics and Easter egg hunts on the lawn; snowmobiling; and Dad and Mike painting cars in the barn, etc. Matthew spent hours in the old barn with his poppop (whom he called Pops as he got

older). Dad gave him leftover wood, nails, and a hammer, and his imagination helped him create lots of interesting things. One time he even built a small shed.

When my children got old enough, they also went on trips with Dad in his 18-wheeler semi. Matthew, especially, loved Poppop's truck.

One of the wonders of Michigan is the beauty of the freshly fallen snow that looks like diamonds in the sun. My family and I loved all of the outdoor, winter sports. By this time, Bumpy and Mike were married and had families and snowmobiles of their own. I would snowmobile with them late into the night, often crossing the nearby frozen lakes. When my brothers and Dad showed up at our door unexpectedly and Dawnie and Matthew heard that loud, familiar roar of the big machines, they would scream with delight. "Mommy, can we go? Please?" And of course, their uncles and Poppop could never get away without them. Mom didn't like the snowmobiles because she was afraid someone would get hurt. I never worried though, because I knew Dad and the boys would guard their niece and nephew with their lives. Dawnie and Matthew would return with rosy, red cheeks, and I would often invite everyone in for hot chocolate and homemade snickerdoodles.

It wasn't uncommon for it to snow so much that all of the schools had to shut down and many of the roads would close for several weeks. My sister-in-law canned and froze a lot of food, and when we couldn't get into town my brother delivered groceries from their freezer to us on his snowmobile. One year, the snow was so deep that when I took a picture of the kids standing in the road in front of our house only their heads were visible. They thought it was exciting to stand in the middle of a busy road where normally they weren't allowed. The snow was about eight feet deep that winter, perfect for building a toboggan run and snowmen in our yard.

In the summer, we enjoyed hours of water skiing on our family speedboat, lovingly dubbed *Barbara Joan* after Mom.

As I reminisce about the many endearing memories of my brothers, two episodes stand out above all the rest. The first is when Jeff invited me to spend a day with him and we made plans to ride all over the countryside on his motorcycle. I borrowed a motorcycle helmet, and off we went. It was soon lunchtime, so we stopped at a McDonald's. The laughter started as soon as I removed my helmet and Jeff saw my ridiculous, flat bouffant. Then, after ordering a big bag of hamburgers and fries, Jeff realized he didn't have his wallet. Instead of getting upset, he simply rested his elbows on the counter, told the sales person that he didn't have any money, and proceeded to laugh

hysterically as only Jeff can laugh. The humor was contagious, and soon I was laughing so hard that my stomach hurt and tears streamed down my face. Everyone was staring at us, but we didn't care because the laughter felt so good. The restaurant workers were so surprised by our reaction that they told us just to take our food and leave! The second memory is when Jeff and I walked all around the quaint town of Coloma on Halloween day, wearing Charlie Brown and Lucy masks. We maintained our composure, which added to the humorous responses from passersby. Jeff always had a way of making life seem brighter and fun, and he could "pick me up" faster than anyone else I knew. A man of few written words, he could make me smile with a sticky note that simply said, "Thinking of you."

I worked full-time as an executive secretary, took private flute lessons, had eight flute students of my own, and was a member of the Twin Cities Symphony and Municipal Band. My life was full. My husband was supportive of my music involvement, and he and the kids attended most of my concerts. It hurt me feelings that Dan's family never had any interest in hearing me play my flute.

The band and symphony were a source of pride for me and technically challenging. I played flute and piccolo in the symphony and sat next to my flute teacher, Charlotte. Perfecting the second part took hours of practice every week. I learned many important things while playing in the symphony: to always have my flute warmed up and be in my chair well before rehearsals started, to listen for intonation, to play with sensitivity, and to never settle for mediocrity.

Matthew was taking Suzuki violin lessons, practicing diligently every day on his quarter-size violin. During one concert, his Suzuki class joined the symphony and performed a technical, classical piece by memory. I was very, very proud.

The Municipal Band performed two concerts every Sunday on the bluff of Lake Michigan in St. Joseph. Local musicians and musicians from Chicago participated in this band. It was an exemplary group, and the director, John Howard, was a kind and unique person. During the five years as a member of this band, there were two highlights for me personally. The first was when the band accompanied me as I played "Annie's Song." The second was when my brother Bumpy was a guest vocalist and sang "It Is Well With My Soul" and "Same Old-Fashioned Way." Gospel vocalists weren't asked to be guests often, so I was particularly proud of my brother. John Howard's wife was critically ill with cancer at this time, and I could tell the words were a blessing

to him. I saw it in his eyes.

Dawnie and Matthew had their first jobs here. They passed out programs, and Mr. Howard paid them each $1.00 per concert. As soon as the concerts began, they headed off to the ice cream parlor to spend their earnings on ice cream cones.

I wanted desperately to be a good mother, and I tried very hard. Too often, though, I hit my children too hard and screamed at them at the top of my lungs. I was taking the anger and hurt from my childhood out on my own precious children. I hated myself for doing it, but I didn't know how to stop.

Dan had a strange sense of humor that I never understood. My brothers thrived on pulling pranks and teasing me, something they had done since I was a little girl. Dan, on the other hand, had an extremely intense, somber personality. Something would be so hysterically funny that my brothers and I would roll on the floor with laughter until our stomachs hurt. Yet Dan would barely crack a smile.

Cabbage Patch dolls were popular, and nearly every little girl wanted one for Christmas. They were expensive, and even though we didn't have much money, I wanted Dawnie to have the opportunity to adopt a Cabbage Patch doll. To my surprise, Dan agreed to purchase and wrap the doll. I could barely contain my enthusiasm on Christmas morning as she ripped the shiny holiday paper and lifted the lid of the box. But what happened next was devastating. Instead of a Cabbage Patch doll, the box held a head of cabbage with a face that had been drawn on with a black magic marker. To my horror, Dan began to laugh. It was hard to imagine that he thought this was a funny joke to play on his little girl. Dawnie and I cried for a long time.

Dan and I had one vacation the entire time we were married. We went to Florida to see Disneyworld and to visit his parents. To earn spending money for this trip, I helped Dad sand a van. It wasn't fun, but I needed the money. Just before we left for our vacation, Dad handed me my first crisp $100 bill and said, "The work you did isn't really worth $100, but since you're my special little gal, I'm going to go ahead and give it to you." It was the first $100 bill I had ever seen!

My brothers did everything for their wives. They were the type of gentlemen who believed that certain chores, like mowing the lawn, shoveling the sidewalk and driveway, hauling wood in and starting a fire, were things for which men were responsible. To my disappointment, Dan was content to let me do these things most of the time. I didn't mind doing these tough chores, but it embarrassed me to admit that my husband was lazy and hurt

my feelings to acknowledge that he didn't love me enough to do the things for me that most husbands did for their wives.

I often mowed the lawn because Dan said he was allergic to the grass. When he occasionally mowed the lawn and had to borrow a mower from one of my brothers, he always returned it with an empty tank of gas, the opposite of what I had been taught. It made me wonder where his parents were when he was growing up. I also did most of the work in our big garden. We purchased a used wood burner to save money, and Mike installed it for us. In the winter, I cut wood with my brothers and Dad. I enjoyed their company, and when I helped, the wood was free. At 6:00 every morning during the freezing, winter months, I started a fire in the wood burner after Dan left for work so that our house would be warm when our children got up at 7:00. I was afraid to light matches, so it was challenging. For several years, that wood burner was our only source of heat. When I had a day off from work, Dan would call me and ask if I would shovel the driveway so that he could get in when he arrived home from work. It was a long driveway, frequently covered with one to two feet of heavy snow.

I did everything for my husband, even at the risk of hurting myself physically. And he never gave it a thought. I was trying to earn his love and looking to him for my self-worth, just as I had done for so many years with my dad....

Seventeen

The Adulterous Affair

We had a loving marriage for 12 years. Although we were different and didn't always agree, I thought we were in love and that our marriage would last forever. We had made a commitment to each other and to God to remain faithful till death do us part, and I took that commitment seriously.

But in 1982, everything began to fall apart. Dan and my youngest brother's wife Marla worked at Leco Corporation, and Dan told me that he would be working longer hours during the week and sometimes on Saturday. What was strange, though, is that his paycheck didn't get any bigger—not too difficult for even a non-math person like myself to figure out. After noticing that they were spending a lot of time together, especially during family get-togethers and church functions, I became concerned. I kept noticing special looks and affections that were being exchanged, the kind between two people who have been intimate. One time was especially obvious. During a Thanksgiving dinner at my parents' home, Marla cut her finger and Dan immediately rushed to her side to comfort her. Then, he drove her to the hospital to get stitches. It was now obvious to me that their relationship was more than just a brother-in-law/sister-in-law friendship.

I questioned Dan, and he did his best to convince me that they were just friends and that I was being suspicious. I wasn't convinced though and discussed my suspicions with Tim and several family members. No one wanted to believe that this could happen in our family.

Mom later told me that she suspected they were having an affair because of the way they looked at each other, and she felt badly that she hadn't said anything. She said she was trying to be a good mother-in-law by not interfering, hoping that what she suspected wasn't true. As Mom had done for so many years with Dad, she held her tongue and looked the other way.

Wanting desperately to believe that my husband still loved me and that his relationship with Marla was innocent, I tried to ignore the late nights,

missing money, and recurring suspicions. Dan took care of our checkbook and finances, so I didn't know that he was spending money on gifts and hotel rooms for himself and his lover.

The weekend before Christmas, we made plans to take our children to a unique restaurant for a special holiday dinner. Children were fascinated by the toy train at this restaurant that ran on an overhead track around and around the ceiling, and adults looked forward to the famous hamburgers. The streets sparkled with Christmas decorations and lights, and the air was filled with anticipation as we listened to the carolers and the Salvation Army bells. As always, it thrilled my children to donate a quarter to the Salvation Army. Already dark at 6:00, it was a beautiful winter evening, crisp and clear, with intricately shaped snowflakes falling from the sky—a perfect night for getting into the Christmas spirit.

Without any warning, just as we were about to begin shopping, Dan anxiously announced that he was missing some cash from his wallet. When I asked how much and he said *all*, I immediately reacted and people walking by me stopped and stared. It was my last check before Christmas, and now my children wouldn't have any Christmas gifts. I was unable to speak all the way home and cried myself to sleep that night.

When I told Mom what happened, she gave me her JC Penney charge card and took me shopping so that I could get the kids some gifts. While we were shopping, she asked, "How in the world did he lose all that cash?" He never admitted any wrongdoing, but I was convinced that he had spent the money on some extravagant gift for Marla. Taking money from me was one thing, but taking it from his own children was beyond my imagination.

My brothers found out about one of the hotels Dan and Marla frequented and waited in the parking lot where their cars were parked for several hours, but they never came out. We knew that they were having an affair and that it had been going on for several months. And yet, neither of them would admit it.

Several weeks later, on a Sunday afternoon, Dan informed me that he wasn't going to the evening church service because he wasn't feeling well. The gas gauge on our car was on empty, so he told me to take $5 out of his wallet so that I could get gas on the way to church. When I opened his wallet, a piece of paper fell out onto the floor. Naturally, out of curiosity, I picked it up, unfolded it, and slowly and deliberately read the contents. I cannot express the raw emotions that flooded my heart as I read that letter, written in Marla's handwriting, describing the sordid details of their lovemaking. I was stunned,

and for a couple seconds felt completely detached from reality. I shouldn't have been surprised, because I had suspected for a long, long time. But to suspect and then have the proof explode in my face was another thing!

It was at this moment that I finally understood the shock and grief that Dad's adulterous affairs had caused Mom. How, I thought, had she survived?

I didn't confront Dan then, because our children were present. Instead, I ran out of the house and drove as fast as I could to Bumpy and Shelly's house, a couple miles away. I knew they wouldn't be going to church, because Bumpy was recovering from having his tonsils removed the previous week. Without knocking, I ran in their back door screaming, "They're having an affair. They're having an affair. I knew it. What am I going to do?"

As he was my oldest brother, I looked up to Bumpy and often sought his advice. He and his wife were our best friends, and they tried desperately to calm me down. But I was inconsolable. My heart was crushed. What would I do? Did Dan still love me? Was he going to run away with Marla? How could I tell our children? Did Timmy know?

How do you forgive someone when they have literally shattered your life so badly that the bruises have blackened your heart and soul, when they have stripped you of your self-esteem, and when they have broken your children's tender hearts? Could I ever forgive the unforgettable? Adultery is a painful, life-altering event that can destroy your world and everyone in it, not just your own life. During the next couple weeks, Tim and I endeavored to put the broken pieces of our marriages back together. It was a very, very sad time for our family, with two marriages affected at the same time. The four of us met with our minister several times. I was enraged during these counseling sessions and openly expressed my anger. I called my sister-in-law a whore, the worst form of accusation I have ever used in my life. Dan always looked pathetic and acted like he had no clue what he had done. Tim wanted to hit him, but he didn't.

Unbeknownst to all of us, Marla had a very tainted reputation. While Tim was grocery shopping several weeks later, someone approached him and said, "Tim, did you know that your wife is sleeping around?" Tim now knew the full extent of her severe emotional and mental problems, which we found out later, were the result of her own childhood trauma.

Even worse than their adulterous affair was the fact that they thought I would let them take our daughter. They planned to get married and then ask me if they could adopt Dawnie. I can now understand how and why people are murdered. During a heated argument one evening, I threatened to kill

Dan. He laughed at me, because he knew I didn't know how to put the gun together or load it. "Dawnie and Matthew love me, and neither one of them would ever consider living with you, and no court would ever give custody of our children to you after what you've done," I screamed.

In 1982 on the day after Christmas, I finally had to admit and accept the fact that Dan no longer loved me and wanted to leave me. Dan moved into a shoebox-sized room somewhere, and Dad, Mom, and my brothers helped me pack the belongings of our life. Dad called Dan the scum of the earth and said he couldn't understand how a man could hurt his wife and children. Yes, I was furious with my husband, but Dad's comment made me so angry that I wanted to lash out and tell him that he was no better. I didn't though, because I didn't want to hurt Mom and my children anymore than they were already hurting. Because I had nowhere else to go, I knew I better keep my mouth shut.

Everything was stored in my parents' attic, and Dawnie, Matthew, and I moved back in with my parents. We lived there in the big farmhouse for about one year. I shared a bedroom with Dawnie—we slept in the same beds and used the same bedspreads that Tammy and I had used at 542 Pipestone. I felt as though I had been transported back in time. Matthew had his bed and dresser in one corner of the big attic. It was a fun, sad year for me. Being near my mom made me feel secure. She endured my tearful, emotional outbursts and not once ever became impatient with me. I went to bed every night with the pain and woke up every morning with the same pain. I felt as though I was being kept alive by some kind of invisible machine. I felt hopelessly lost and didn't think I would ever find myself.

Another thing that broke my heart at this time was the sudden, unexpected end of my relationship with my sister-in-law, Shelly. I never understood why she sided with Dan and severed our friendship. When I needed her support, she let me down. While Dan and I were separated, he and Shelly formed a close relationship, so close, in fact, that friends and relatives became suspicious. We found them in several questionable situations but never knew for sure.

During one of the worst snowstorms of the season, Shelly insisted on driving to Kalamazoo to go shopping. The blizzard had created zero visibility, and I94 had been closed for several hours, yet she told Mom that she had to go to Kalamazoo. Dan was working in Kalamazoo at an insurance company. His boss called me that afternoon and asked if I had seen him in the last few hours. "No, I haven't seen him since he left for work this morning. I thought

he was going to Kalamazoo." We found out later that Dan and Shelly had spent the day together.

Bumpy and Shelly eventually divorced, and other than the hurt it caused my niece and nephew, I wasn't affected. Any emotional attachment between Shelly and I had already been destroyed. I never thought she loved Bumpy and felt that my brother deserved better. I don't think Shelly ever truly knew how to love anyone. When I asked her to forgive me for anything I had done to hurt her, she simply stared at the floor with her hands at her sides, showing no emotion.

My family was supportive, and they prayed that Dan and I would get back together and that our marriage would be saved, but Dan's parents offered no support. My father-in-law told me that every man deserved one affair and that I should get over it. I couldn't believe that a Christian parent would make a statement so contrary to Biblical principles. Instead of holding his son accountable, he was making excuses for him. After that comment, I wondered if my father-in-law had broken his commitment and oath with his wife.

I don't know what I would have done without my family during this time. Although my children were heartbroken, they felt secure because they knew that their grandma, poppop, and aunts and uncles were close by. My brothers spent a lot of time with them, and Mom was there waiting for them at 3:00 every afternoon when the school bus brought them home. They played cards and all kinds of board games with Mom and frequently took on the challenge of an intricate puzzle together. Saturday was always popcorn night just as it had been when I was a little girl. Those are treasured memories that we will never, ever forget.

My children looked up to their uncles and their poppop. In their eyes, they were heroes.

I felt ashamed that I had messed up my own life, and this shame caused me to be jealous of my sister. Every time I saw her, she was wearing the most updated, stylish outfits, and I could barely afford necessities for my children and myself—and I mean necessities, like sanitary napkins. When I was on my periods, I took paper towels from the bathroom where I worked and carefully folded and lined my underwear. Tammy had planned a big, beautiful wedding, something else I never had. She worked at Motts Children's Hospital at the University of Michigan in Ann Arbor as a secretary and was engaged to a nurse anesthetist. They planned to move to Galveston, Texas, after the wedding. It wasn't Tammy's fault that she had carefully planned her future.

My reactions were immature and selfish.

I knew I couldn't run from my problems, but the thought of accidentally running into Marla or Shelly created so much anxiety and stress that I was willing to do almost anything to avoid seeing either one of them. I wanted my children to have a better education and had been contemplating a different school system for some time, so it seemed like the perfect opportunity to research the schools and employment in Ann Arbor. I interviewed for my sister's job, was hired almost immediately, and relocated to Ann Arbor in August 1983. It was only three hours away, and yet Mom and Dad were devastated that day as I drove out of their driveway. As they watched and waved from their back porch, I felt like I was kidnapping my own children.

My children were angry and unhappy for quite a few months, because my decision forced them to leave their security and everything with which they were familiar, and they knew they would have to change schools again. They didn't know that my motive for moving was to get Dan back. If I could get him away from Marla, I thought, maybe he would realize that he still loved me and would come back to us.

In my devastation, I turned my back on God and didn't seek His guidance. I was headed for destruction, and my well-organized plan didn't work. It takes two to make a marriage successful, and although Dan did eventually move to Ann Arbor and into our apartment, he did so under false pretenses.

The obvious signs, like the fact that Dan didn't have a driver's license and wouldn't explain why, that he had no desire to have sex with me, and that he couldn't get a job, should have been warnings that there was something terribly wrong. Although I did not know it at that time, there were other things going on in Dan's life that were negatively affecting his ability to make rational decisions.

But because I still loved him, I chose to look the other way. We were still legally married and there was a tiny glimmer of hope in my heart.

I tried to support the four of us on my $17,000 secretarial salary, but it wasn't enough. One weekday morning when I went outside to start my car, it was gone. "My car's been stolen right out of the parking lot," I said out loud. When I went back into our apartment and told Dan, he looked at me with a smirky grin and said, "It was stolen, it was repossessed!" Our rent was always late, and the apartment management tried to evict us several times. Even though Dan wasn't working, he always had an excuse to avoid going to court with me. Facing the apartment representatives and their attorneys by myself was nearly unbearable and intimidating, and I almost always broke down

and cried. It was disappointing, because I knew I was doing the best I could with the income I was making.

There are several happy memories in my life that are so moving they are stamped on my heart forever, never to be forgotten. Likewise, there are unhappy memories that are so painful I wish I could erase them from my mind. Following are several of those unhappy memories:

The executive for whom I was working asked me to fly to New York to assist him with a Chapter 11 on a business there. After working 11 hours two days in a row, I was exhausted and decided to go to bed early—it was about 9:30. As always, I made sure my hotel door was locked. I'm a light sleeper, so the noise outside my door woke me up immediately. All of a sudden the door opened and the executive walked in and closed and locked the door behind him. "What are you doing in here and how did you get in here?" I screamed. It was instantly obvious that he was drunk, and although I couldn't understand everything he said, I was able to understand it when he said he paid a hotel clerk to get the key to my room. He tried to get into my bed, but I screamed louder. After a couple minutes that seemed like an eternity, he left. I didn't hesitate for a minute. I got dressed, packed, called the other woman who had been working with us, asked her to help me get a flight out of LaGuardia Airport and to pick me up as soon as possible. Within an hour I was on my way back to Michigan. The next day I went to the CEO of the company and told him what had happened. I also told him that if the executive wasn't fired immediately I would press charges against him and the company. The CEO acted very swiftly, and I never saw that executive again. Justice was served, but nightmares haunted me for a long time afterwards.

Because of my financial problems, grocery shopping was an impossible challenge—what to put in the cart, what to leave out, what we wanted, what we needed, what could we do without, did I make a mistake in the addition on my calculator, etc. One Saturday, as I stood at the checkout counter waiting to have my groceries rung up, my son asked if he could have a candy bar. "Of course you can, honey," I reassured him.

And then it was my turn. I was paying cash for my groceries, and as I watched the register total continue to climb with the scanning of each additional item, I became more and more nervous. Realizing I wasn't going to have enough money, I began to mentally decide what I could put back. I tried not to panic. Then, the total! Although I cannot remember the exact total or amount of cash I had, I clearly remember that I was short several dollars. With an innocent, serious expression on his little face, Matthew, age

ten, looked up at me and said, "I can put my candy bar back, Mom." A kind gentleman in line behind me offered to make up the difference—I think he may have been an angel. The embarrassment I felt was nothing compared to the lump that welled up in my throat at my son's unselfish offer.

Our minister operated a feeding program at our church, and every week someone on his staff put a big box of food together for us. The kids knew there would be treats tucked in somewhere—granola bars, fruit, cookies, etc.

During one of my counseling sessions, our pastor told me that Dan was "rotting on the vine." I didn't completely comprehend his comment, but I slowly began to understand that Don did not love me and had only come back to me because he couldn't get a job and had no place to live. I finally got enough courage to tell him that if he didn't go to counseling with me and get a job, he would have to leave. He was waiting for an excuse and wasted no time packing his things to move into a room at the YMCA.

I will never forget that day. The look on Matthew's face as he watched his Dad leave for the second time pierced my heart. As Dan struggled to get away, Matthew lay on the floor with his arms wrapped around his daddy's legs, holding on as tightly as he could. With every movement of Dan's legs, Matthew's rigid, grief-stricken body dragged behind. It gripped every part of me.

The months of wear and tear caused by the emotional, mental, and physical trauma of enduring my husband's adultery and his rejection finally ended. The marriage was dead. He had killed it. I filed for divorce and asked God to help me make a new beginning for my children and myself. I was strong, like my mom, and I knew that we would make it with God's help and the support of my family and friends.

The Court awarded me weekly child support of $45.00 and gave us joint custody. I was left alone every other weekend when Dan took our children away. I missed them desperately, and because of my loneliness and vulnerability, I made wrong choices. I met a much younger, good-looking guy where I worked, and after several group parties we began dating. During this time, I often spent the night with him at his father's house, leaving my children all alone. I knew they weren't old enough to be left alone, but I allowed my selfish desires and lust to take over my common sense. I seldom attended church and often went out on Saturday nights to a local bar and restaurant to dance with my boyfriend and some of his friends. One night, I had several mixed drinks. Since I had never consumed alcohol, with the

exception of an occasional glass of wine, the two glasses of Coke and Rum made me drunk. The bar was across the street from my apartment, and I couldn't even make it home by myself.

I remember looking up at my daughter, then 15, from my prone position on the bathroom floor the next morning. As she looked down at me and kicked me slightly to show her disapproval, she said, "I don't feel sorry for you, Mom." Her reaction was justified. It was one of the most embarrassing, humiliating moments in my life. It never happened again.

My boyfriend was an assistant cross-country coach at a nearby high school, and since my children were both in cross-country and I was running also, we often ran together in the evenings and on the weekends. Running kept me in shape and relieved my anxiety and stress. To my surprise, after working for many weeks to improve my speed, I won an award for the second fastest time in my age category in the 5K Pumper Power road race. My children were proud of me as I stood on the platform and accepted my medal.

My family disapproved of this relationship because my boyfriend was much younger than I and didn't share my same religious beliefs. I knew that sex outside of marriage was wrong, but I thought of everything to justify my actions. I had been stripped of my self-esteem and needed and craved the attention I got from this younger man. I was confused. I thought he cared about the kids and me, and I thought I had strong feelings for him as well. But it was lust, not love. When I finally made the decision to end our relationship, I walked into his house, told him I could never see him again, and walked out. I never saw him again.

It's a miracle that I didn't get pregnant, and I thank God for protecting me. It took courage to let my boyfriend go, because he made me feel like I was beautiful and special—the same feelings I had yearned for when I was a little girl. The incest from my childhood had caused me to look for acceptance and love in the wrong place. Incest continues to cause destruction for many years, even after it stops.

Thank goodness God never gave up on me. I loved my Heavenly Father with all of my heart and knew that He had been waiting patiently for me to come home. I thought about my future and wondered what it would be like to meet a wonderful Christian man and fall in love. He would have to be an extraordinary person who would love my children as much as he loved me. I began earnestly praying for God to fulfill the desires of my heart. He often does this for His children....

Eighteen

Finding Happiness

In 1986, Mom and Dad began building their dream, a cedar log home. We were ecstatic that at age 59, our parents were finally getting their first new home. We had hours of fun in the tiny, one-bedroom apartment they rented while their home was being built.

They worked all day at their full-time jobs and then worked on their log home every evening. Everyone pitched in, and my children and I spent many weekends in Benton Harbor helping them. Mom and I installed the insulation on a 90-degree summer day. My brothers, already master craftsmen, worked many, many hours on this house. When it was finally finished, it was an exquisite log home, with open exposed beams in the living room, a hardwood floor in the kitchen, and country blue carpet throughout the rest of the house. This was Mom's first new carpet, and we all enjoyed walking on it barefoot. I was deliriously happy for her.

Unfortunately, happiness doesn't always last. Soon after they moved into their new home, Dad did something embarrassing and terrible. He always wore thin, white boxer shorts around the house, the kind without snaps on the fly, and when friends of our family and their teenage son came to visit one day, this is what he had on when he answered the door. He invited them in but made no attempt to put any more clothes on. Then he sat in one of the wingback chairs, put one of his legs up on the arm of the chair and proceeded to subtly rub his crotch. Mom said she noticed the young boy, obviously confused, kept looking back and forth, first at his parents, then at Dad, and then back at his parents. It was a humiliating slap in the face for Mom. She wanted to speak up, but she was afraid. I could hardly contain my anger when Mom told me what happened. Little did we know what the future held.

My children and I had been attending a church in our neighborhood because it was only a couple blocks from our apartment. They wanted to go back to our former church in Ypsilanti, but it was a 30-minute drive from

where we lived in Saline and I told them I couldn't afford the gas for two trips every Sunday. The real reason was due to a frightening experience I had gone through with one of my female friends while we attended church there. She invited me to go to a movie with her one Friday, but instead of driving to the theatre, she took me to a secluded place, turned the car off, and locked the doors. She had been having some marital problems, and I thought that maybe she wanted to talk to me before we went to the movie. Then she reached over and put her hand on my upper thigh. "What in the world are you doing?" I said.

Her response was chilling. "How do you know you won't like it if you don't try it?"

I asked her to take me home immediately. When I got home, I called a Board member from the church and told him what happened, and he assured me that the situation would be handled by the pastor. It was a terrible shock. Although I never knew how it was handled, she and I never spoke to each other again.

A few weeks later when my friend Betty called me and said she wanted to introduce me to their friend Joe, my curiosity was sparked. So, in June, we visited our former church. We sat in the very front row, and during the praise and worship service Betty pointed him out to me. His eyes were closed, and his hands were raised toward Heaven. His face looked kind, and his hands masculine, yet gentle. I knew I wanted to meet him.

Many weeks later he told me that when he looked down and saw me that Sunday morning he thought I looked like an angel. I wasn't even aware that he had noticed me, and I'm sure he didn't know about Betty's plan to introduce us. His mom was visiting from Illinois that day, and as I walked past her and said hello to him, he turned to her and said, "She's going to be my next wife." Evidently, when he saw me sitting with my children, he assumed that I was single. Or, perhaps the Holy Spirit had spoken to his heart.

At the end of the evening service that same day, I went to the altar to pray. All of a sudden, I felt a hand on my shoulder. Someone was praying for me. When I turned around, Joe was standing there. "May I have a hug?" he asked tenderly. We still had not officially been introduced, and yet I felt that I already knew him. I could discern that he was a wonderful man, and he smelled so good—he was wearing Stetson.

After the Wednesday evening service, he came up to me again, and in the most delightful hillbilly accent said, "How come you're so pretty and I don't know your name?" It was a line I had never heard before, and I was skeptical,

but to my surprise he was genuine. We began talking on the telephone late into the night and spending lots of time together. "Mommy has a boyfriend. Mommy has a boyfriend," Dawnie would sing.

He took me to a little hole-in-the-wall joint on our first date. When we got there and I saw the run-down condition of the building, I was offended. This was our first date and I thought he should be trying to impress me. "This place makes the best pinto beans and cornbread, and you're in for a real treat!" After our delicious meal, I knew he really was trying to make an impression. Never had I eaten such awesome pinto beans, cornbread, and coleslaw. Carl's Diner soon became our favorite restaurant.

Joe was meticulous. The first time I went to visit him at his apartment, I had to laugh when he opened the door. There were no footprints on the carpet, and it stood straight up like it had just been vacuumed. He kept a small plastic rake by the door, and any time he left his apartment he raked himself out so that there would be no footprints. And this man wanted to date a woman with two teenagers? I was lucky if they made their beds every day! A couple weeks after we met, he came to my apartment to pick me up. As soon as he entered the back door, he asked if I had some cleaning solution and a rag. "Why?" I asked. "So I can clean the top of your refrigerator," he responded. To ease my embarrassment, he quickly explained that he knew I was too short to see the top of the refrigerator.

Dawnie and Matthew joined us during many of our dates, and the four of us spent a lot of time in the swimming pool at his apartment complex. They enjoyed eating out at restaurants, and because it was such a novelty it was hard for them to decide what to order. They would go over and over the menu until we told them they had to make a choice or they wouldn't be eating anything.

One of our dates was very humorous and quite unforgettable. Joe took me to an outdoor, Christian drive-in theatre, and in the middle of the movie I started kissing him passionately. He tried to ignore me, but I was persistent and told him that if he didn't reciprocate I was going to go into the back of the van and take all my clothes off. He looked at me and in the most quizzical tone of voice said, "You're going to do what?" Needless to say, humor quickly replaced the seriousness of the moment, with Joe breaking out into hysterical laughter. And yes, I had to repent.

Joe and I were both born-again Christians and very serious about our relationships with Jesus Christ, and we both loved music. Joe was already in the choir, and I joined the alto section soon afterwards. We formed many

close friendships with the choir members who were like one big, happy family. I played my flute in the orchestra and occasionally accompanied the choir on the piano. Both of us auditioned for solos in the Easter cantata, and, to our surprise, were both selected for solo parts. I'm not sure who was more frightened, but I know I was shaking just before I had to sing my alto solo, "See Him in the Garden."

I was in love with Joe but was concerned about his two previous marriages and the distant, dysfunctional relationship he had with his only child, a daughter. I was also upset about his vasectomy, because I yearned for another baby. And yet, there was no doubt in my heart that God had brought us together. We weren't perfect, but we were perfect for each other. After dating for only a couple weeks, Joe asked me to marry him. Although I would have been content with a simple gold band, he gave me a lovely diamond engagement ring and diamond and ruby wedding band. We soon made plans to drive to Eldorado, Illinois, over the Labor Day weekend to meet and visit his parents, Ruth and Walter.

Several days before leaving for Illinois around 7:00 in the morning, I heard a siren in the distance. Dawnie had only had her driver's license a short while, but since I wasn't going to work that day I told her she could drive the car to school if she took Matthew to his early morning band rehearsal. The siren caused me some concern, although I reassured myself that my children were safe. About one hour later, I heard the telephone ring. Now I really began to worry. The siren and now the telephone—this couldn't be a coincidence. Sure enough, it was the hospital calling to tell me that my children had been in an automobile accident. Sensing my concern and fear, the nurse immediately assured me that they were going to be all right. When I hung up, I quickly called Ford Motor Company in Wayne, Michigan, telling them it was an emergency and asking them to have Joe Rutherford paged. The drive from Wayne to Saline normally took about 30 to 40 minutes, but that day Joe made it in 25 minutes. By the time he got to our apartment, my ex-husband was at the hospital with our children. Even though the car was almost totaled, Dawnie and Matthew sustained only minor cuts and bruises. When I saw the car, I knew God had protected them.

They were badly shaken, and Dawnie was hysterical. Matthew said she was crying because she was afraid she was going to get in trouble—a typical sibling comment. She had turned left directly in front of an oncoming car, and she knew she had been careless. I was so thankful that they weren't injured that I couldn't bring myself to punish her. The lesson she learned that

day was punishment enough.

My children stayed with friends the next weekend while we went to Illinois. Joe's Mom worked at a little dress shop, and I will never forget what she said to me when I walked in the door. "Oh, they're here, they're here, and I think I'm gonna squall." I wasn't familiar with the word squall, so I wasn't sure if it was good or bad. I was relieved when she explained that she was so happy she thought she was going to cry.

Mom and Dad Rutherford extended Southern hospitality to me to the fullest extent, and from the very beginning I felt very comfortable in their home and knew that they loved me. Dad Rutherford found out that I craved ice cream, and he spent an entire afternoon churning homemade vanilla ice cream for me. I only knew him a short time. He died a year later after an abrupt illness with cancer.

Our associate minister, Pastor Fish, agreed to marry us, but only under the condition that we attended marital counseling. This is when I told Joe that I had been the victim of incest for many years. His face portrayed sadness for me, but he didn't seem to want to talk about it further at that time. During one of the three sessions, our pastor asked if we had engaged in sexual activities yet. With a proud voice, I answered, "Of course not." Joe was quick to respond though. "We haven't had sex yet, but Jody has tried to talk me into it several times!" Pastor Fish laughed so hard he nearly fell off the chair. I was relieved to see that he had a sense of humor, although my face turned red with embarrassment.

We were married on December 12, 1987, in the farmhouse that Joe had rented for us in Milan, Michigan. My friend Betty created a warm, homey atmosphere with Christmas lights and candles, and it looked beautiful. In his smooth tenor voice, Betty's husband, Dan, sang "If." Our music pastor's wife, Karen, played "Somewhere in Time" on the piano, and our dear friend, Pastor Fish, performed the ceremony. Even with a migraine headache, my sister-in-law Sharon coordinated the refreshments and cleanup. A few close friends and relatives, my children, Joe's daughter, and my mom attended the candlelight ceremony. Joe wore a brown wool vest and suit, and I wore an ivory lace, tea-length dress and silk derby hat. From the time I entered the room, he never took his eyes off me. And oh, the love that those eyes displayed as he beheld his bride—you would have had to be there to see it. After an informal reception with homemade apple cake, Christmas cookies, punch, and coffee, we were left alone to enjoy a short two-day honeymoon. I was ready to start the honeymoon, but Joe told me he couldn't "perform" until he

was fed. So, off we went to a nearby restaurant.

We were in love and so thankful to have each other. We had both been through painful divorces, and to have another opportunity at happiness was a special blessing.

We spent many wonderful months in that old farmhouse. It had one tiny bathroom, squirrels in the walls, and fat, furry spiders in the basement. Matthew and Joe took their showers under a hose rigged in the middle of the basement. In the evenings, we took long walks in the woods, sat out on our homemade swing, or watched the deer romp through the cornfields. It was so peaceful. And almost every evening during the summer months, we drove into town to get ice cream cones. This is the summer that Joe nicknamed me Fluffy.

I only had one sad memory while living in the farmhouse. My son, Matthew, would dress up in Army fatigues and play splat gun in the woods. Many times, he would sit on the front porch steps for hours waiting for his dad to come and play with him—sometimes he would sit out there until it was dark. It was heartbreaking for me to watch him, because we knew his dad wasn't coming. It was especially miserable for me, because it took me back to the many times when my brother Mike used to sit on the back steps at 522 Pipestone Road waiting for my dad to take him fishing—Dad hardly ever showed up. Broken promises!

Joe had stomach ulcers when he was a child, and these ulcers escalated into more serious complications. When I married him, he had already been through seven or eight major stomach surgeries, ultimately having most of his stomach removed. I had to endure several surgeries with him after we were married, and although I knew that God would protect him, watching him suffer was very stressful. He seldom complained, and to this day, after suffering through many serious illnesses and surgeries and being close to death several times, he remains optimistic and tries very hard not to let any circumstance take his joy away.

Joe was a strict disciplinarian, but he was fair. He came into my life at a time when my children needed a role model and someone whom they could trust. It wasn't always easy, but I made every effort to support him during the times when he had to be confrontive and firm. Joe bragged on my children and spent many hours on his knees praying for them. They may not have always agreed with him, but I know they loved and respected him. He was one of the first people in my life to whom I looked up and respected and who really lived like a Christian. He practiced what he preached and seldom

compromised, and he mixed this with tons of compassion and love.

Because Joe had not been involved in his daughter's life after she turned 14, having an instant family was a new experience. Being the stepfather to two teenagers could have been quite stressful, but he took it in stride. He was proud of them and sincerely wanted to be involved in their lives. He attended every cross-country meet and every band concert even when I couldn't. He disliked the cold Michigan weather, but during football season he faithfully endured the freezing temperatures while watching Matthew and his friends march in the Saline Marching Band. When Matthew had a trumpet solo, Joe and I would almost bust with pride. He teased Matthew by saying that he was going to bring his electric blanket to the games.

It takes a great deal of humility for anyone to say, "I'm sorry." Whenever Joe felt he had made a wrong decision or had been too hard on the kids, he'd go to them and ask their forgiveness. It blessed me more than I can tell you, and I am certain it meant a lot to them as well. There were times when we had to painfully use tough love on our children, like the time Dawnie abused the use of her first credit card and ended up in serious debt. Although we both felt terrible, we knew we couldn't help her. She had to pay off the debt herself in order to learn how to control her spending. Watching her apply her entire check toward her credit card debt week after week was emotionally exasperating, especially when she didn't have any spending money.

Together, we endured Dawnie's boyfriends, one, in particular, who was a bitter, unhappy teenager. He monopolized the television by watching sports, forcing Joe and I to feel like we had to leave our own home. Once, during dinner, he threatened to stab Dawnie with a fork. We realize now that we were the parents and should have usurped our authority and asked him to leave. In fact, we should have discouraged the relationship from becoming so serious. Unfortunately, parents don't have any experience before they have to deal with these complicated situations. We and our children made some serious mistakes and paid dearly for them, but we have forgiven each other and know that God has forgiven us.

Nineteen

The Ugly Secret is Exposed

As we were getting ready to walk out the door to leave for church one beautiful Sunday morning in May 1988, one week before Mother's Day, the telephone rang. I couldn't imagine who would be calling us at this time on a Sunday morning. After all, our family and friends knew we would be on our way to church. Fear flooded my mind as I prepared myself for the possibility of bad news.

"Hi sis, it's your brother Mike." I quickly explained that we were getting ready to leave for church, a 25-minute drive, and that I would call him back later. "I have to ask you a tough question that can't wait until later," he somberly interrupted. By the intensity and seriousness of his voice, I immediately knew that we would either be late for church or would not be going at all. I could sense that our conversation was going to be lengthy and serious. I tried to calm myself knowing that this was my serious brother.

"Sis, I don't know any other way to ask this question, but did Dad ever sexually abuse you?" Why in the world, I wondered, would he be asking me such an appalling question, and why couldn't it wait? For perhaps one of the few times in my life, I was at a loss for words. After a moment of silence, he spoke again. "I have to ask, because I just found out that Dad molested one of our nieces. She told her parents that Pops did something to her that she didn't like. She said he touched her dubie."

Mike often acted as the spokesman for our family, so it was not unusual for him to do so in this situation.

I began to cry as I desperately choked out bits and pieces of what had happened to me. "Yes, yes," I answered sensitively. "Dad molested me for many, many years." All he could say was "I'm sorry, Jod, I'm so sorry. I never knew."

From the front porch of the old farmhouse where I was standing, I could see my husband and two children, then 15 and 17, sitting at the kitchen table.

The questions on their faces were so obvious. I knew I had to give some explanation for the shock that was so evident on my face, but my lips could not form the words. The horrible secret and all the years of suffering were finally being exposed and uncovered. Feelings of guilt engulfed me as I realized that my sweet, precious niece had been sexually molested by someone whom she loved and trusted. I never dreamed that Dad would sexually abuse his own granddaughter, an inexplicable thought considering he had also abused his own daughters.

After a few seconds, Mike asked, "Does Mom know?" With great hesitation, I answered, "No, Mom never knew!" By this time, I was in serious condition emotionally. My heart began to pound and I couldn't breathe. I wanted to transport myself through the telephone so that my brother could hold me. I felt a frantic need to be with my brothers and sister. "I love you, sis. I will call you back this evening after I have a chance to talk to the boys and try to decide what to do and how to tell Mom."

How could we tell our mom that her husband had sexually abused her daughters and granddaughter? She knew that Dad had committed adultery, and she knew about my brother's beatings with the belt, but she had no inclination whatsoever about the sexual abuse.

I didn't even know that Dad had abused my sister until she told me in 1977. She told me that although Dad had never had sexual intercourse with her, he had done other things to her that were terrible.

I shouldn't have been surprised, but because I didn't understand how a sex offender's mind worked, it never occurred to me that Dad would start molesting my little sister after I was out of the house. Leaving home to go all the way to Springfield, Missouri, in 1969 to attend college was my chance to break away from Dad's abuse and control.

So many questions: Was there any way to spare our mom this grief? How would we tell her? How would I make her understand that I couldn't tell her when I was a child because I was afraid of Dad and was threatened not to ever tell the "secret"? Would it take away her will to live? Would Dad finally realize that he had been wrong and had caused irreversible pain and grief? Should we call the police? Should we give Dad a chance to help himself? How was our little niece holding up? Should we prosecute?

As we said good-bye and I realized that I would have to tell my own children, years of suppressed emotions and grief exploded into confusion and weeping. My heart and soul were crushed. I felt like my physical body was detached from my heart and mind. Although I did not realize it at that

moment, the process of healing and restoration in my life was beginning. I already knew that I was the Lord's special daughter and that He wanted to heal me—I just had to get that reassurance embedded into my heart.

Twenty

The Arrest

The look of tenderhearted compassion on my husband's face made me cry more, and my children's reactions are stamped on my memory like a tattoo. My son, not given to tears often, began to cry. My daughter, often prone to emotional outbursts, simply stared into space as if she could not possibly comprehend what she was hearing. Surely it can't be true, they thought.

They were still coping with the heartbreak of my divorce from their dad several years earlier, and now I was telling them that their grandfather had committed horrible acts of abuse.

My children were the first two grandchildren in our family, adored and loved by their grandparents. My parents lived each day for them. Now, the two men whom they loved and trusted most, their dad and grandfather, had let them down. I was grieving for my children and myself. How could I help them when I didn't even know how to help myself?

It was painful enough for all of us to learn what had happened to our niece, but to add to that all four of my brothers found out for the first time that Tammy and I had also been sexually abused. Remembering my brothers' beatings with the leather weapon and all the times they were sent to bed without dinner made me weep bitterly, like it was happening all over again. Their abuse seemed so much worse than mine. Sometimes revenge feels good, and successfully sneaking dinner to them was a major victory every time. I used to run to my bedroom and hold my hands over my ears in an effort to muffle their screams while Dad was torturing them with his belt. The beatings seemed to last forever, and I was always afraid that he would kill one of them or break their arms. "Stand still while I spank you or I'll break your arm!" he would shout unmercifully. I would beg God to make him stop!

The next three days were a nightmare, filled with sleepless nights and

continuous telephone calls to and from family members, friends, and pastors. We wondered how those without church families coped. My family and I were going through every emotion imaginable. As our tears flowed unashamedly day and night, we held tightly to the promise found in *Psalms 30:5: "Weeping may endure for a night, but joy comes in the morning."* The nights were so long and the suffering so severe, that we questioned whether our joy would ever return.

I felt like my life was over. I didn't know if I could survive. My body seemed to be in reverse. The pain was so great that I could not eat or sleep. I became constipated and for several weeks could not even have a bowel movement. I didn't want to live. Living meant I would have to see and feel Mom's pain. Yet I knew my own precious husband and children needed to see that I had the will to survive.

Dad was never a Godly example, but taking us to Sunday school and church and making us read our Sunday school lessons definitely paid off. We knew the scriptures and knew that God, who was bigger than any problem, would get us through this horrendous nightmare. Sometimes, when an unexpected situation catapults you into a tragedy, you simply have no choice but to lean on the arms of Jesus Christ. The devastation is so great that you cannot make rational decisions without His help.

Before our decision was final, Mike met with the new pastor for coffee at a local restaurant. After explaining that Dad had sexually molested one of his grandchildren and asking for guidance, Pastor Dan said, "As a minister, it is my responsibility to let the law know." This frightened Mike, because he now realized that we could no longer turn back. And yet, it was the confirmation that we needed. Mike then told the pastor that he would speak with an officer of the law. Indeed, it was too late to turn back. The time had come to make Dad accountable and to get him the help he needed.

My sister and youngest brother, living in Texas and Florida respectively, made plans to fly home immediately. Joe and I arranged for our children to stay with our friends, Dean and Linda, and we drove to Benton Harbor with plans to meet the rest of our family at my parents' home on Wednesday evening.

We asked Chuck Longnbarger, a state policeman and family friend, to confront Dad in the parking lot at his place of work. After several unsuccessful attempts to meet Dad, Officer Longnbarger left his business card on Dad's truck. By now, Dad sensed trouble and could feel that something was coming down. He finally called Chuck, only to find that his suspicions were right.

Dad was a long-distance truck driver, and when he returned from his trip that Wednesday afternoon, Chuck met him and escorted him home so that he could be there when Dad broke the news to Mom. We asked Chuck because he knew our family well and understood how much we loved Dad. He also understood that we wanted to show Dad that we were serious and meant business, short of pressing charges. Chuck handled Dad as a friend that fateful day.

Little did we know that the whole ordeal had to be reported and documented. Chuck spoke to the Court on behalf of our family, and this seemed to weigh heavily in our favor regarding the manner in which we wanted to help Dad. Although Dad thought that we were all out to get him, every decision we made was made with love and with Dad and Mom's feelings in mind. At all cost, we did not want to cause any more pain and suffering, especially to Mom.

Both of my parents worked at Leco Corporation in St. Joseph, Michigan, Dad as a long-distance truck driver and Mom as a crucible inspector in the factory. Without knowing, they both left work at 4:00 that afternoon and ended up in their driveway at the same time. Mom waved to Dad from her car as she always did when he returned from a long run, and she noticed that there was another car behind Dad. When they all got out of their cars, Dad said, "You remember Chuck don't you, Barb?" Mom responded by saying hello and that she remembered him. "*We* have something to tell you," Dad said. Mom's initial reaction was that something must have happened to one of their children, so her maternal instincts immediately surfaced.

When they got inside, with Chuck standing on the opposite side of the room from Mom, Dad told her that he had sexually molested one of their grandchildren. At this time, Mom was unaware that Chuck's purpose for standing opposite her was so that he could see her expression when Dad told her—he wanted to know for sure whether or not she had ever been aware of the sexual abuse. (Chuck explained this to Mom several months later.) The instantaneous, stunned expression on her face confirmed his suspicions. She never knew.

And then, the appalling reality of what had happened to me when I was 13 hit her! I hadn't been raped by a stranger, but by my own father. Suddenly, many unanswered questions now had answers. "You were the one who raped Jody, weren't you, John?"

Although I was not there at that moment, I am sure she felt as if her heart had been ripped right out of her chest. After surviving:

- years of financial stress,
- years of mental and verbal abuse,
- years of rejection,
- years of knowing that her husband had been unfaithful,
- years of living with a drunk husband,
- years of not knowing where her husband was when he didn't come home,
- years of seeing her children mistreated and whipped,
- years of not having enough money to provide for her children,
- years of not having friends because of Dad's immoral, irresponsible behavior,
- and years, so many years, of embarrassing and shameful gossip,

now she was hearing words that she could hardly believe. Surely it wasn't true—that her husband, whom she had forgiven over and over again and whom she still loved, had sexually molested her daughters and granddaughter. Sometimes grief is so intense that the human soul cannot react. I believe this was how it was with Mom that day. In a desperate and hopeless attempt to protect her mind, body, and soul from the consuming anguish, she froze, unable to cry or scream.

As Dad retreated to the bedroom, my brothers, sister, some of their spouses, and Joe and I began to arrive. As each child walked through the door, Mom said she felt as though she were receiving flowers at a funeral. Indeed, the shocking news was like a death, too frightening and painful to comprehend. I can still see Mom's face as she sat on the piano bench—stiff and hard, almost mask-like. She couldn't respond. She couldn't speak. She couldn't cry. She couldn't even go to God. He had to come to her.

Several minutes later, we heard an unexpected, horrifying scream. We ran to the bedroom to see what was wrong and found Dad on the floor on his knees screaming like a wounded animal. He looked like someone who had been stripped of every ounce of dignity. Dad had always controlled everything we did and said. To see him out of control was nearly unbelievable. We thought maybe he was having a nervous breakdown and were confused and sympathetic, hoping that maybe, just maybe, he finally realized the seriousness of what he had done.

Together, as a family, we cried and talked that evening for many hours. While sitting on the green couch, Dad made a feeble attempt to apologize to me for what he had done. He had his arm around me, and it made me very uncomfortable. I desperately wanted to believe that he was sincere, but thoughts of doubt filled my mind. Was he truly remorseful or simply ashamed because he had been caught and his sin had been exposed? Could he ever change?

He didn't understand the impact of what he had done—abusing and raping his daughters and then molesting his granddaughter. Or, perhaps, as is the case with many perpetrators, he was in denial.

As we began leaving, we agreed to meet at Mike's home on Saturday morning to pray together. Prayer changes things, and we were determined to intercede for our family. Most importantly, we knew that we had to break the cycle of child abuse in our family.

During the next couple days, we got together often. Always thinking of others, my sister-in-law, Lori, had a fresh pot of flavored coffee ready. During one of these times, we decided to purchase a new Bible for Dad. We were trying so hard to be optimistic. Dad had not been prosecuted yet, and we felt that this was a beginning—an appropriate time to give Dad a new Bible. We had no idea that it would take more, much more, to change Dad than simply giving him a Bible.

It was a warm, sunny day as we gathered together on Mike and Lori's big country porch with the antique wicker furniture, the same porch that held so many beautiful, unforgettable family memories: birthday parties, high school graduation open houses, baby showers, Father's Day and Mother's Day celebrations, Memorial Day picnics, etc.

We all signed the Bible and presented it to him on Saturday morning during our devotional time. We took turns emptying our hearts of our disappointment and grief, and we made a heartfelt attempt to encourage Dad, Mom, and each other. "Why did you do it, Dad?" I asked over and over. He didn't respond. He only shrugged his shoulders.

The statute of limitation for my sister's abuse and mine had long passed, but my niece's molestation could still be prosecuted. Penetration with any object, for which Dad could have been convicted, is a first-degree sexual offense in Michigan and punishable by many years in prison. Dad seemed to be genuinely sorry, and because we wanted so much to believe his sincerity, we made the decision to ask the court for leniency so that we could try to get him help.

A telephone call was made to Chuck to inform him of our desire to ask the prosecuting attorney to allow us to work with our dad toward healing and restoration. The thought of prison doors slamming behind him was more than we could handle, and since we were such a close family, we were confident that we could work through the problems. Unfortunately, we were naïve and did not and could not have possibly understood the enormity and seriousness of Dad's addiction to sex and pornography.

The prosecuting attorney agreed to give us the opportunity, with the promise that Dad would abide by our conditions and seek counseling. We told Dad that he had to quit taking long-distance runs so that he could get off the highway, even if it meant losing his job. Dad had a serious addiction to sex and pornography, and we knew that the long-distance runs created a constant source of temptation. We also told him that he had to quit drinking, attend church, get counseling, and read his Bible faithfully. Mike even went to Dad's boss, the president of the company, several times to convince him that Dad needed a local driving job.

At this time, Mom had been nominated for the "Mother of the Year" award at our church, and all too soon we remembered that we would have to face a congregation of friends we had known for many, many years. Until now, only our pastor and a few close friends were aware of what had happened in our family.

The following letters (unedited) from my siblings and myself tell why we felt our mother should receive this award:

I WOULD LIKE TO NOMINATE: Barbara Enders, 600 Hillandale, Benton Harbor, MI AS "MOTHER OF THE YEAR"

I BELIEVE SHE SHOULD RECEIVE THE HONOR FOR THE FOLLOWING REASONS:

Mom has had many blessings in her life: six kids, many grandchildren, all healthy. She has also had many hurts and disappointments. Through the good and the bad, she has remained one of the most steadfast Christians I've ever known. I've always told her that I think she's a saint, and she says, "Oh, I'm one of the farthest things from a saint." But when a person always has time for counsel, praying with you, listening to your heart, helping you carry your sometimes heavy burdens and uplifting you with Bible readings, what more can be said. I think that she epitomizes the "words" that the Bible has

set down as a Christian woman and mother, and I will always praise God for her friendship and Christian fellowship and for being my mother.
YOUR NAME AND RELATIONSHIP: Bump Enders, Son

I BELIEVE SHE SHOULD RECEIVE THE HONOR FOR THE FOLLOWING REASONS:

Raising six children in a Christian home is a remarkable accomplishment. Mom made many sacrifices for us to ensure that we were taken care of, loved, and given the opportunity to have musical instruments. She did this alone for many years, because our father wasn't saved and gave her little support. Because of her sacrifices, faith, and endurance, all six children are serving the Lord and are using their talent for Him. Even though we didn't have much money, she made sure our home was filled with security and love. She always had the perfect combination of discipline and patience, and she stood by us and supported us through all our trials. She has remained sincere and tenderhearted, even after suffering physically and enduring devastating situations in the marriages of three of her children. Mom is a strong woman and believes in the power of prayer. She rises every morning at 4:00 a.m. and spends time praying and reading her Bible before going to work. She does not gossip, but always only kind words of others, and she is respected in her home and at work for being honest and hard working and for being a Christian woman who loves the Lord. I love, cherish, and look up to my mother. It is my desire to grow spiritually so that I can be the Mother and Grandmother that she is.
YOUR NAME AND RELATIONSHIP: Jody L. Rutherford, Daughter

I BELIEVE SHE SHOULD RECEIVE THE HONOR FOR THE FOLLOWING REASONS:

Since Mom gave her heart to the Lord some 25 or 30 years ago, she has been steadfast in her faith, often without Dad by her side. Through all the trouble Dad caused her years ago, she still held strong to the Lord and insisted on keeping her children involved in church. Contemplating twice a divorce due mostly to Dad's drinking and fighting and a near loss of my life (also due to his drinking), she still stuck with him and continued to love him and does to this day. I've asked myself why did she? Wives wouldn't go that far today; they would just divorce. Mom had a nervous breakdown when we were kids. It's no wonder with six little brats and a husband that couldn't find his way home some nights. God brought her through these valleys only to gain new

heights. We were not well to do by any stretch of the imagination, yet every Christmas we would take needed supplies and gloves to a particular black family around the block. We didn't lack for love; we had plenty of that. She taught us how to love and even to have a greater love for members of our own family, as we are today a very close-knit family, although some miles apart now. We never were taught that there was a difference between race and color. If we were to cut down or gossip, Mom was quick to cut that off and suggest we talk about something encouraging and uplifting. Mom has never been one to gossip, only to speak good of. As we have had two divorces in our family, you will not hear Mom talk badly against them; she still loves her daughter-in-law and son-in-law as if they were still a part of our family. You talk about a mother and a God fearing and believing mother to love and look up to—they don't come any better than her. Mom looks little and maybe weak, but yet she is so strong and mighty, yet soft, sweet and tender inside. She fought the devil from our front steps many times and many times alone. Her love for God is quiet, prayerful, and very patient. She is the finest Mother a child could have. As I dated several girls, it was no chore in deciding on a wife, because I wanted a girl just like the girl that married dear old Dad, and of course, I have one as you all know. One day maybe Lori will be "Mother of the Year," but for now Barbara Enders, my mother, should be voted this honor, for she has gone far beyond the limits of being a Mother and Wife— if you only knew. Whether she receives this award or not, the biggest and most longed for reward will be her mansion in heaven, and knowing that all her family will someday help occupy it there with her.

YOUR NAME AND RELATIONSHIP: Mike Enders, #2 Son

I BELIEVE SHE SHOULD RECEIVE THE HONOR FOR THE FOLLOWING REASONS:

Although we six kids dished out disappointment after disappointment during our raising years, Mom's love and faithfulness never wandered for us! Crushing setbacks in our personal lives revealed on the heels of financial and other problems, and still Mom stood strong. Again and again we six kids challenged her strength and level of tolerance with a bombardment of, "kids just growing up" situations and demands that seemed intolerable. She would say, "I'll always be here and always be right behind you." And thou the tears came like rivers some times, Mom stood strong, relying on God and simply trusting God. Yes, the tears came and with them new strength seemed to come also. On, what a Mom. She raised six kids, who at times I 'm sure were

not angels, and it probably seemed as if we didn't appreciate her, but we really did. She is truly loved and respected as a leader and also a spiritual leader. The six of us still go back from time to time to draw on the gentle but persevering courage of a real woman of God, each time coming away settled and sure. She raised us while under extreme personal pressure and still had time to make a house a real home. She instilled in me a gentleness and caringness and affection that I'm very proud to carry, and a love for God and country that I hold high and dear, a real treasure that I shall never forget or neglect. This year, 1987-1988, has been another tough year in our family, and Mom, although very quiet and reserved, has fought the battle like a real trooper. She's come out on top, again and again, to be a shining light to her family. She's a beautiful woman, and I love her dearly.

YOUR NAME AND RELATIONSHIP: Jeff Enders, a very happy and loving son.

I BELIEVE SHE SHOULD RECEIVE THE HONOR FOR THE FOLLOWING REASONS:

Mother of the Year should not reward one mother but all mothers. Being a mother is a God given talent and each bundle of joy she receives is a gift from God. God is not a respecter of persons or mothers, therefore, man shouldn't look to one individual as the best. I'm 30, and for the first 14 years of my life my father drank. As a child growing up, my mother would always make sure we went to church. She was always eager to have a family altar time and still is. Mom always seemed to have a kind and encouraging word for me. I can remember her saying that I was special because God made me. I didn't fully understand that as a child, but now I know I was chosen before the foundations of the heavens and earth were laid. She was indeed right. My heavenly father does love me as much as she told me and more. Mom had a special place to pray, in Grama's rocker. I can remember many days when I would pop in unexpectantly seeing her interceding for our family with the Bible in her lap. I'm sure she prays there today. It was not easing raising six children with little money, but Mom always had a good meal on the table and Christmas presents under the tree. Although we may have been considered poor, we were rich with the blessings of a caring mother. During the last year, Mom has gone through a lot. I would talk to her on the phone and feel the hurt in her voice. The pain that she has endured is only by the grace and love of Jesus Christ. Our family is a tight knit family, and we owe it all to Christ. Regardless of whether or not she gets this reward, I know her true

reward will be in heaven.
YOUR NAME AND RELATIONSHIP: Your #5 Son, Timothy Elliott

I BELIEVE SHE SHOULD RECEIVE THE HONOR FOR THE FOLLOWING REASONS:

She raised six children through extremely adverse conditions, i.e., she had a nervous breakdown when I was 5 and my father was an alcoholic until he was saved when I was 12. She instilled in my brothers and sister and I high morals and values that I can never, never thank her enough for. My mother is a "quiet" Christian woman who loves the Lord dearly. I have seen her help people and pray for them in a way that only one who as been there can. I have heard of many sad, sad relationships between mothers and children, but not so in our case. Besides my precious husband, my mother is my absolute dearest friend. She's open, honest, and caring, and I have been able to talk to and share with my mother every aspect of my life. The highest compliment I could ever give to my mothers is that if I could ever be just a fraction of the woman, wife, and mother that she is, then my life would truly be worthwhile. I love her with all my heart and miss living near her—it makes the times we are together so special. Every child probably thinks their mother should be given this special honor of "Mother of the Year." In the hearts of the six Enders children, Barbara Enders will be "Mother of the Year" every year to us. She epitomizes the phrase "Mother of the Year."
YOUR NAME AND RELATIONSHIP; Tamara Enders Hamelink, Daughter

Home was and still is Benton Harbor to me. Whenever I went home, it was customary to play in the church orchestra with my siblings. So, on Mother's Day, as always, we went to our orchestra seats at the front of the church. With unsteady hands, I put my flute together and joined my brothers and sister. Several times during the praise and worship service as the congregation sang, I had to put my flute down. I couldn't play. I couldn't pray. I could only cry. I didn't know how long I could hold up.

Finally, Mom and our entire family were called to the platform of our large church. As Joe and I walked hand in hand alongside the rest of my family, my legs became weak. My throat was so dry it felt like it was stuck shut. I felt sick to my stomach. My heart was pounding so fast I was sure someone could see the pulsating in my chest. Though we were often an emotional family, I am sure that some members of the congregation could sense that we were in a severe state of grief and shock. The fake smiles on

the faces in the photograph that was taken that day reveal the sleepless nights, tears, and strain—hardly a normal reaction for an award ceremony.

As Pastor Dan presented Mom with the "Mother of the Year" plaque and the congregation stood and applauded, I realized, perhaps for the first time, just how much she truly deserved this tribute. Even though we could not fully celebrate the honor that had been bestowed on her at that moment, we knew it was God's perfect timing. Although Mom felt that some other mother was more deserving, as she so often did because she was so humble, I knew she needed this gift and recognition. Indeed, our entire family needed the affirmation.

With Dad and her family at her side, she accepted the compliments and award with dignity and honor, forcing a smile of appreciation on her face. It was a strained, fake smile, but nevertheless, a smile, with the corners of her mouth turned up ever so slightly.

Later that day, as Dad leaned against the kitchen counter of their home, he asked Mom if she could ever forgive him. With strength in her voice as powerful and resolute as the angry seas of a hurricane, she said, "I don't know if I can ever forgive you, John, but if I ever do, it will take a long, long time."

It broke our hearts as we all began to leave to return to our own families and homes. I was afraid to leave Mom. I wanted to protect her. And yet I knew that she and Dad needed time alone to communicate their feelings privately. As I hugged and kissed them both good-bye and told them I loved them, I prayed that God would give them the grace and strength they would need to make it through the next few days and weeks. I had no idea what the future held for them. I could only pray that commitment, time, and love would somehow heal the wounds. I knew they needed a miracle.

Back in Ypsilanti in my own church, I cried through every service. After each service ended, I couldn't wait to escape. I literally ran from the pew to the car, leaving Joe and my children behind. The horrendous grief and sadness had migrated from my heart to my face, creating a homely, oppressed look on features that used to radiate with joy and happiness. I didn't want anyone to look at my tear-stained face. I didn't want them to ask me any questions.

Photographs

Jody Lynn, age 3 1/2

Grandma Flossie and Jody, age 6

Jody, age 13

The Enders Family, November 1958
Back row, left to right: Jeff, age 5; Timmy, age 17 months; Barbara (mom), age 29;
Bumpy, age 9; Jody, age 7
Front row, left to right: Mike, age 6; Tammy, age 3 months

Family Picture, 1968
Front, left to right: Mom, Tammy, Dad
Back, left to right: Mike, Jody, Bumpy, Jeff, Timmy

Southwestern Michigan Junior Miss Competition, 1968
Jody, age 17

Junior Miss Competition, 1968

Family Photo, June 1976
back, left to right: Dad, Mom, Band Director Bernie Kuschel
front, left to right: (in age order) Bumpy, Jody, Mike, Jeff, Tim, Tam

Jody and Joe and their wedding day
December 12, 1987
"Sealed with a kiss!"

Matthew and Dawn in 1990

My precious mom and siblings, Christmas 2000
front, left to right: Mike, Tim
back, left to right: Jeff, Tam, Mom, Jody, Bumpy

Todd, Grant, and Dawnie
Jody's son-in-law, grandson, and daughter at Grant's 1st birthday party

Matthew and Katrina
Jody's son and daughter-in-law

Jody and Dot, 2002
Performing at a wedding reception

Buddy

Jody, Joe, and Scooter, February 2003

Twenty-One

The Prosecution and Violent Fight

In May 1988, when we found out that Dad had molested our niece, to early 1990, Dad made no effort toward restoring family relationships or changing his attitude and lifestyle. He was still in serious denial and still very bitter that his crime had been exposed. He continued to tell Mom that he didn't understand what was so terrible about what he had done. After all, he tried to reason, the sexual abuse hadn't caused any physical pain!

During this 18-month period, Mom went to work faithfully every day even though she rarely made it through an entire workday without crying. Sometimes, while inspecting crucibles on the assembly line, she would start crying and wouldn't be able to stop. Then one of her friends would tell her to go to her supervisor's office. He was a mutual friend of Mom and Dad's and aware that something alarming had happened in our family. Mom was normally strong emotionally, so it was unusual for her to lose control at work or any other place. But every human being has their limit, and Mom had nearly reached hers—the walls were beginning to crumble. She would go to Fred's office, stand there and cry, and Fred would simply say, "Go home, Barb." Even though he didn't know what was going on, he recognized that her grief was so overwhelming that she simply couldn't continue to function. Grief and depression has this effect.

We knew that if Dad wasn't made accountable for his crime, he would probably continue to abuse and molest children. We also knew it was our lawful responsibility to report the sexual abuse to the proper authorities. Still, it was an agonizing decision. After much deliberation and prayer, we, as a family, made the decision to have Dad arrested. Although he didn't know of our decision right then, Dad could feel something coming down, and he was getting very nervous. "I'm getting out of here, going to North or South Carolina!" he shouted at one point. He said his children were trying to control his life and call the shots, and he became furious. Mike and Dad had

many tough conversations, and Mom pleaded with Mike to stay away from him. "He'll beat you up," she warned.

We called on Steve, a state police officer and family friend who had always liked Dad. Though it felt cheap and underhanded, we informed Steve where Dad would be getting his haircut that morning. Because we suspected that Dad might go crazy and possibly try to fight, Steve took a backup officer. Dad's older brother Don was with Dad and knew what was going to happen. When Dad left the barbershop, the state police vehicle pulled up behind Dad's car and stopped him. Dad immediately knew what was happening and told his brother that it was the end of his life. "No, John, this could be the first day of the rest of your life," his brother responded.

Dad didn't resist as he was arrested and handcuffed. Uncle Don drove Dad's pickup truck home.

What a terribly, terribly sad day for all of us.

The following article was printed in *The News Palladium* on July 3, 1990:

Man gets probation in fondling case

A Benton Township man who admitted fondling an 11-year-old girl two years ago was sentenced Monday in Berrien Circuit Court to five years probation. John A. Enders, 61, 600 Hillandale Road, also was ordered by Judge Casper O. Grathwohl to avoid contact with children except in the presence of another adult and to obtain counseling. He was credited for eight days already served in jail. In May, Enders pleaded guilty to a reduced charge of attempted second-degree criminal sexual contact with a relative in April 1988 at his home. He later withdrew the plea because Grathwohl did not follow part of the plea agreement recommending no additional jail time. At the original sentencing, Grathwohl ordered Enders to serve 90 days in jail and complete a long probation term. Enders later dropped the withdrawal after his attorney conferred with the judge.

Several days after the article appeared in the newspaper, Mom went to work as usual. She didn't want to go, because she knew that many of her co-workers would probably have read the article. She managed though, because her children's prayers had empowered her with courage and strength. When she arrived, her two dear friends, Betty and June, were waiting outside in the parking lot. As she had suspected, they had read the tragic news. Because they cared about Mom so much, they wanted to support her by walking into

work with her. That's what good friends are for—to hold you up when you can't stand on your own.

I understood what Mom was going through. When Dad was arrested, my emotional state became so unstable that I eventually had to take a couple weeks off from my job. My supervisors knew what I was going through and were very understanding and supportive.

After Dad was arrested, one of the first things Mom did was burn his boxer shorts. During his nine days in jail, several black men in Dad's cell kept using horrible, trashy language. Dad, of course, threatened them all. Profanity offended Dad and yet he thought it was okay to rape his daughters.

Every time the telephone rang, we all fell apart. Dad was calling collect, and we desperately wanted to answer the telephone and hear his voice and know that he was all right. But we couldn't. He had to be accountable for the things he had done, and we had to be brave. Dad called Mom so much that she finally had to quit answering the telephone. When it rang one time, my sister said, "It's Dad again, calling from the slammer jammer." Even during tragedy, God gives us humor, sometimes in the most unexpected ways.

He begged to be bailed out of jail, but because it was a holiday weekend and the courts were closed, he was forced to stay in longer. I believe Dad's younger brother Stub finally paid the bond. He was the only brother who disagreed with how we had handled the situation, and he was very angry with all of us, especially Mike. Strange though—for a long time after this he didn't want anything to do with his favorite brother. As children and young adults, they were inseparable.

Dad couldn't reach anyone for a ride home after he was released. However, Tammy found out he was getting out and finally reached Mike, and he agreed to pick Dad up. When he arrived at the jail though, he was told that Dad had already been released. Mike soon found him walking down Pipestone Street, many miles from his rural home. Mike could see that Dad's feet hurt after walking so many miles, and he felt badly for Dad. Mike parked his truck on the side of the road, locked it and said, "If you're not riding with me, then I'm walking with you." It was an act of compassion that Dad didn't deserve.

Such a long, tough walk home. We thought we had removed all of the guns from Mom and Dad's home, but Dad assured Mike that we hadn't. Dad talked a lot of junk and hinted of suicide if we didn't leave him alone. He used his manipulative skills and threatened suicide when it seemed to be convenient, saying he was going to drive his semi off a mountain. Another attempt at guilt trips and manipulation.

The following reactions are word-for-word statements that were submitted to the Victim/Witness Services during Dad's court proceedings:

Victim's Personal Reaction

This has devastated our family. We are an old-fashioned, very close-knit family. When one hurts, we all hurt, as we do carry each other's burdens.

I called all my brothers and sisters together and explained what happened. I then notified Dad's three brothers and sister. All of us were in agreement that he should be turned into the law and that he needs professional help. At present, we are more concerned where he is heading than where he has been.

This has been the toughest time yet for our family, and it has been stressful on us all. Our niece is very intelligent for her age, and we feel she has a real good grip on this. Counseling for her has been suggested by several, if even for only one time. She has not been taken to counseling yet. However, when this is all over, her family will consider taking her for at least one appointment and more if necessary. Of course, she does not want to go. She only wants this to be over with and behind her.

Comments and Concerns to Express

We all love Dad. It's true we have lost some love, respect, and trust for him, but hopefully, with hard work and determination, he will gain that back. From the beginning we never intended for him to serve any jail or prison time, though we did know that this was a strong possibility. We do not feel prison would be the answer for him now. He is soon to be 62 years old and will be able, when he is ready, to retire from Leco (as a truck driver of 15 years). We are in hopes that Leco will continue to employ Dad. We are almost certain they will. We would, however, like to strongly suggest these recommendations:

1. To be on probation with steady counseling as often as and for as long as the court deems necessary.
2. We want Dad off the highway and driving locally. Absolutely no more "over the road" driving or long hauls.
3. No bars and no drinking.
4. We also think it would be a great idea for Dad to read books, as if

he were the victim, so he can slowly begin to understand what he has done and how the victim must feel. One such book: Pain and Pretending.

5. We would like to recommend a counselor that works out of South Bend. If it were our choice this would be our decision: Dr. Clint Gabbard, 300 N. Michigan, South Bend, IN, 219-287-0762.
6. Possibly community work would be in order.
7. As a last resort, instead of jail or prison, I would like to suggest Teen Challenge in Muskegon, MI, Phil McClain, 616-798-7927. They have done a great deal of work in helping rehabilitate people of all ages with this type of sickness.

Our whole family is in total agreement with these recommendations. We will all (including his brothers and sister) help Dad, back him, support him and pray for him. We love him and we would hate to have to lose him. Please give our suggestions a great deal of thought. We are all ready and patiently waiting to help him. Thank you very much.

Sincerely, Michael A. Enders, March 29, 1990

Comments and Concerns to Express from a Family Member

My concern is what might happen to Dad now. I don't feel a prison term would help him at all. I love Dad, and despite what he's done would like to see him get steady counseling for as long as necessary in order for him to turn his life around for the better. There is a list of recommendations expressed on Mike's letter. They are too lengthy to list again, therefore, because I am also in agreement with these recommendations, I ask you to consider them with much thought.

Reaction of Victim's Mother, March 29, 1990

This has been the most difficult thing I've ever had to go through. Not only because my precious daughter was involved, but also because a person whom we loved and trusted betrayed us. The impact this has had on us as a family has been great. It's been something that has weighed heavy on our minds these last two years. We can hardly get together with the rest of the family and not discuss Dad and this whole situation. It makes those times very stressful, and because Dad has not made a real effort to change or get help it just compounds it. It is my

prayer that one day we'll all be able to put this behind us and finally get on with our lives.

Victim Impact Statement, March 28, 1990
Victim's Name: Name omitted at victim's request
People v: John Adam Enders
Case #: Criminal Sexual Conduct-2nd
Victim's (my niece's) Personal Reaction: I wish it had never happened.

I feel nervous every time I am around him. Every time I have to talk about it I get really scared. I hope what we are doing will help him and everything will be back to normal again. Even though all this has happened to me, I still love Pops. I really hope he gets help and doesn't go to prison. Like I said before, I hope, someday, everything will be back to normal.

Shortly before Dad was convicted and prosecuted, Mom and Dad gave their depositions. While Mom was being questioned, she could see Dad out of the corner of her eye. Each time she responded to one of the interrogatories, she could see him shaking his head in denial. She knew he was disagreeing with her responses, but she knew she was telling the whole truth and nothing but the truth. They were, after all, under oath, and Mom considered that oath a serious commitment to state the facts without exaggeration. Dad was a master at lying and manipulation and no longer knew how to tell the truth. After their depositions were taken, he looked at Mom and said accusingly, "How could you do this to me?" There was no hesitation with the resolve in her declaration as she said, "How could you do this to us?"

Perpetrators don't want to take responsibility for their own actions and often try to blame someone else, usually the victim. Dad unsuccessfully tried to blame his eight-year-old granddaughter by saying that she was aggressive for her age. Denial is a dangerous thing, and Dad was in deep denial.

Telling her parents took great courage, and we praised our niece for knowing, at her young age, to tell someone. It was extremely hard for her, because she said that what Pops did to her was very icky. Just before the sentencing, Dad threatened that he would take it to trial before he would go to prison, hoping that we would back off. He knew a trial would result in our niece having to testify, and he knew that we did not want her to have to go

through any more trauma. It was Dad's last-ditch attempt to manipulate, control, and put himself first.

Although I don't know how it happened, there was no trial. At the Berrien County Courthouse in St. Joseph, Michigan, on June 7, 1990, after the attorneys plea-bargained, Dad was sentenced to 90 days in jail and five years of probation. I attended the sentencing, along with Mom, most of my siblings, and some of their spouses. When the court clerk announced People v. John Adam Enders, fear engulfed me. As I watched my dad, in handcuffs, being led by an officer into the courtroom, I began to cry. I knew he had been in the county jail awaiting sentencing, but to see him in handcuffs like a common criminal was desperately heartrenching, almost incomprehensible. Conflicting emotions stirred within me during the sentencing. Yes, he had committed terrible crimes, but he was still my dad and I felt sorry for him and still loved him. An unfamiliar black woman sitting behind me, filled with compassion and sensing my grief, put her hand on my shoulder at one point during the sentencing. In response to her gentle, subtle touch, I reached up and placed my hand on hers. At that moment, I felt an incredible strength flow into my body. Perhaps she was an angel.

During the hearing, Dad's attorney spoke in favor of him and said that drinking had never been a problem in John's life and that all his family wanted was for him to go to church, or something to that effect. A shameful and terrible lie! The judge didn't buy any of this though.

As Dad stood before the judge, Mike endeavored to speak on behalf of our family in between frequent outbursts of emotionalism and tears. I don't know how he made it through his letter that day. He told the court that drinking had always been a problem with Dad and that the drinking made his volatile temper even worse. Before the judge and the entire courtroom, Mike's tender, broken voice portrayed staggering love and support for Dad. No one that day could have disputed the commitment, forgiveness, and unconditional love that we had for Dad. Even the judge responded by telling Dad that he had never seen such a remarkable family so willing to support their father in lieu of what had happened. He also told Dad that many families would have disowned, killed, or washed their hands of their father. I remember similar words from the judge: "Mr. Enders, when you start taking full responsibility for what you have done, then, and only then, will you receive any empathy from this court."

Before the verdict was pronounced, the judge asked Dad if he had anything to say to his family. The words that came out of his mouth were unbelievable.

"I don't have a family any more," he whispered in a barely audible voice. I felt like he had died and that I had lost him forever. I knew without a doubt that our decision to prosecute was the right one, but for the first time I realized that it was irreversible.

As long as I live, the image of my dad walking past me as though I no longer existed, eyes staring at the floor, hands secured behind him in handcuffs, a man in captivity being punished because he had abused and betrayed his own grandchild, will never, ever vanish from my heart or memory.

Dad could have been sentenced to 15 years of prison, but because of family intervention with letters and support, the court gave him only five years of probation. During this probation, he was not allowed to hunt, drink alcohol, or vote.

After Dad was convicted, he was fired from his job immediately and lost all of his benefits and insurance. Without his income, Mom couldn't afford to keep the beautiful log home. The devastating words "FOR SALE" were now displayed on a sign in the front yard of the home she loved. Dad packed some of his belongings, left the log cabin, and rented a tiny one-bedroom home from friends down the street.

For several weeks, Mike had been hearing Dad's version of what had happened from Dad's friends. This version was, of course, far, far from the truth, and it made Mike very angry. Sometimes anger is justified, and this was one of those times. Mom was very concerned and warned Mike to stay away from Dad. "He'll beat you up if you provoke him, Mike," she warned.

Mike went to see Dad. When he knocked on the door, Dad answered and said, "You came to cause trouble didn't you?"

"No, Dad, I don't want to cause trouble. I just want to talk to you." Mike tried desperately to talk to Dad in a civilized manner, but it didn't work. Dad grabbed Mike and tried to throw him out of the house, and then Mike pushed Dad over the corner of the dryer. When Dad got up, he hit Mike twice in the head with his fist. Although I do not understand why, Mike let Dad hit him. Again Mike tried to make Dad understand that he had not come to fight. Hard to believe that this was Dad's favorite son, the one who had stuck by him through thick and thin.

Dad turned to go back into the house, and Mike told him no, not until we talk. This is when Dad went on a rampage, shouting all kinds of profanity, then busting Mike's lip open and continuing to attack him like an animal. Mike really thought Dad wanted to kill him, and he probably did. Dad couldn't stand up to the truth, but he had to know it inside.

In Mike's own words: "However, by this time, the Lord was no longer with Dad, He was with me." Twice Dad swung at Mike and missed. Mike did not want to hit Dad, but he had to defend himself. He hit Dad several times in the head, busting the skin open. Now completely out of control, Dad continued to come at Mike like an enraged animal, causing both of them to lose their balance. Mike knew he couldn't go down on his back with Dad on top of him, so he pushed Dad as hard as he could. As Dad started to stand up, Mike began punching him—right, left, right, left, grunting with all his weight, strength, shoulders, and anger. Mike was a man of slight stature, and as with David when he killed the giant, God had also been with my brother.

As Mike was hitting Dad, he remembered all the crap and beatings that Dad had inflicted on himself and his brothers and sisters. He was hitting Dad for them as well as himself. Victory only lasted a minute though. He could see that Dad was out of breath, bleeding, and seriously injured, and now he felt badly and so very sad. "Dad, let's stop." Mike then picked Dad's hat and watch up off the ground and handed them to him. Then, with remorse in his voice, he said, "Dad, leave our family alone and stay out of our lives."

With a bloody face and swollen hands, Mike returned to work only to be given a three-day layoff for fighting. His boss never knew what really happened.

Dad later told Bumpy that he was surprised that Mike could hit so hard. When I saw Mike's hand in a cast a week later, I immediately knew that Dad had forced him into a fist fight, because I knew Mike would have never started a fight. It took a full year for Mike's hand to heal.

Dad eventually called Pastor Dan and told him about the fight, and Mike, realizing that he had fought with his own father, began to wear and tear on him emotionally. He soon found himself writing a letter of apology to Dad. Dad taught all of us to take a lickin' and then get up and go on. In other words, be quick to fight and argue but then apologize and get on with things. And that's exactly what Mike did.

I am so proud of my brother. Through this entire brutal ordeal, he displayed compassion, forgiveness, and wisdom.

Twenty-Two

Trying to Heal and Moving to North Carolina

In 1991 Matthew joined the Army. When he left for basic training, I felt like my heart had been ripped out and didn't know how I was going to survive this initial separation from my youngest child. As he was walking to get on the airplane and turned around for one last look at his family, I saw tears in his eyes. Those tears broke my heart. I was concerned because I thought that he had made a mistake and that the Army wasn't God's will for him. He was only 18 and had never been away from home for an extended period. Joe was very patient and prayed daily for Matthew and me. It was a trying time, but with God's help we made it. I believe Matthew learned some valuable lessons that influenced his future, and I learned how to give my son back to God.

Joe, I, and an Army captain friend flew to Missouri to attend Matthew's boot camp graduation. When I first saw Matthew, I was shocked at how much weight he had lost. I was so happy to see him that I couldn't stop hugging him. While his battalion marched and sang their cadence, I ran right alongside them. Joe was concerned that I would embarrass Matthew, but I didn't care. I was his mother, and all of the tears I had shed earned me the right to do whatever I wanted to do. Joe and I were so proud of Matthew that we were sure the smiles were permanently etched on our faces.

When we returned from Missouri, I found out that Mom and Dad's home had been sold and that Mom was moving into the attic of Jeff and Mary Sue's big, historical home until she could decide what to do. Although I was not there, my sister told me that it broke her heart and Mom's heart the day they drove away from the log home. They were afraid to look back lest they crumble. Mom managed to dig up some of the beautiful Trillium plants that she loved with hopes of planting them in a new yard some day.

God puts the broken pieces of our lives back together, and sometimes, when a piece seems irretrievably lost, He gathers what He can and continues to restore us. Since 1988, my family and I have attempted to put the shattered

pieces of our lives back together, individually and as a family. Some of those pieces may never be retrieved, and yet we continue to strive toward healing. We have each had to go through the agony and pain in our own way, sometimes struggling to get through one day at a time. We used to get together often and laugh and have fun, but after the horrible secret was exposed, we could no longer talk to each other or spend time together without hashing over the sordid details. It controlled every conversation and every family holiday. Although sometimes repulsive, these verbal debates helped me heal.

During the years that my dad was molesting me, I survived by turning the sexual touches into the hugs and love I needed. The years of childhood abuse affected me profoundly, and at times the grief and fear was so relentless that it caused unbelievable stress, insomnia, nightmares, fatigue, constipation, and nausea. A broken spirit caused the fatigue. The nausea was the product of worry. The loss of appetite was the root of sorrow.

Joe wore Stetson cologne, but for some reason he decided to try Old Spice one time. When he walked into the house and I smelled it, I instantly became hysterical. He was shocked and couldn't understand my reaction. Dad wore Old Spice, and when I smelled it on Joe, I was catapulted back to the nightmare. On one of my days off from work, Joe came home and found me sitting on the floor hiding behind a recliner crying. "What are you doing here, honey?" he asked.

"I'm hiding so no one can hurt me," I stuttered between sobs. I always tried to maintain a poised, professional demeanor no matter how I felt inside, so for me to be sitting on the floor behind a recliner was very disturbing to my husband. Joe got down on the floor and sat with me until I was under control. He didn't try to reason with me—he just listened as all kinds of unpleasant, hideous things spilled out of my mouth. I needed someone to hold me and listen, and because he loved me, he knew exactly what to do.

Joe literally loved and prayed me through these long months of grieving. It must have been very painful for him—newly married for six months, adjusting to a new wife and teenage stepchildren, and then being submerged into this family horror. Sometimes tragedy rips a husband and wife apart. It drew us closer.

I knew that a confrontation with my dad was crucial, so one day I called him. When I heard his voice, old fears surfaced and I immediately began to shake. "Hi Dad, it's your number one daughter (N1D) calling to ask if you would consider letting me sit in on one of your counseling sessions." To my astonishment, he agreed. During this costly 90-minute session, for which

Dad paid, the counselor encouraged me to openly and freely verbalize my anger, disappointment, and hurt. I was brutally honest, but I never lost control. During the entire session, Dad's face hung to the ground, and he wouldn't look at me. As he had said to me so many times in the past, I wanted to scream out, "Look at me when I'm talking to you!"

When I was a little girl, sometimes I sat on Dad's lap while we watched television. I distinctly remember one particular hour of local news. There was a blanket over my lap, and while Dad was rubbing my nibber under the blanket the news commentator was talking about a man who had sexually molested a little girl. In his customary cocky tone of voice, Dad aggressively said, "How could anyone do something like that?" During our counseling session, I reminded him of that time. "Dad, you rebuked that man for doing exactly what you were doing!"

Dad's counselor told him that my anger was justified, and I could see that Dad didn't like her comment. I could sense his humiliation. When I left that day, my burden had been lightened. Before leaving, I hugged Dad and told him that I loved him. And I meant every word from the bottom of my heart. He knew.

The counselor eventually issued a report to the state, advising that she would have to quit counseling Dad because she could no longer help him. Even this professional counselor couldn't get through to him.

In March 1994, Joe retired after 30 years of service as a hi-lo driver with Ford Motor Company. He was loved and respected at the Wayne Assembly Plant, and his friends and supervisors gave him a wonderful retirement party, complete with a decorated cake with the Ford logo, a sentimental card, and gift of money. Nearly every person on his shift signed his card. I attended that party with him, and watching so many big, strong men cry touched me deeply. He didn't preach to his friends, he just tried to be a Christian example.

After his retirement, we relocated to Walnut Cove, North Carolina, so he could help his sister care for their aging mother. The first six months were very, very stressful. Having to leave my children, then 21 and 23, was almost unbearable. I felt empty and alone. I didn't want to be in North Carolina, and my unhappiness soon turned into anger and bitterness toward my husband. He made me move away from my entire family, and it was his fault that my children and I were suffering.

Matthew adjusted quickly, possibly because of his busy college/work schedule. But Dawnie had an unbelievably difficult time. Every time we talked on the telephone, we both cried. She was getting ready to have major

breast surgery, was recently engaged, and was planning a big wedding. She needed her mother, and I needed her.

I was extremely emotional at this time and cried uncontrollably without any notice. I cried every time I talked to my children on the telephone, every time I wrote them a letter, every time I received a letter from them, and when something reminded me of them. When I saw Matthew's favorite orange drink in the grocery store, I cried. To make the situation worse, I felt like I had to hide my true feelings from Joe because he didn't understand what I was going through.

I had to go to work right away because we couldn't survive on Joe's retirement pension, so I accepted a temporary position supporting several high-level executives at a large bank in Winston-Salem. While working, when I could no longer hold back my emotions, the tears would fall from my eyes and leave white streaks on my cheeks. Many of my co-workers had experienced what I was going through, and they knew that crying was part of the healing process. Again, during the first six months in North Carolina, I went through yet another trying situation. Our daughter was scheduled to have necessary breast reduction surgery. She had assured us that the procedure was not serious, so Joe and I had not made plans to be with her. However, right after the surgery we received a telephone call informing us that the six-hour procedure had been serious and that our daughter was crying for her mother. I nearly fell apart. My supervisor called me into his office, asked me what was wrong, and gave me permission to leave and get on the first airplane to Michigan.

Even though I wanted to be with my husband and loved him very much, I continued to blame him for moving me to North Carolina. I didn't think I would ever get over being separated from my children. It still hurts, and I still miss my family, but I have learned that my contentment and peace come from my Heavenly Father, whether or not my children are absent or present. During our first year in North Carolina, Dad and his female friend showed up where I worked. He was on a long-distance run from Michigan and thought he would stop to see me and introduce me to his friend Betty who lived in Charlotte. When I saw him, my first reaction was to hug him, because I had missed him and still loved him very much. In the middle of the lobby right in front of the receptionist, I started to cry. After I regained control, Dad, Betty, and I drove to a nearby restaurant.

It was one of the most uncomfortable situations I have ever endured. Dad told me about his church and that his girlfriend was a Christian. I love to eat,

but I was so nervous I couldn't swallow. I couldn't be myself. After lunch, in the new home Joe and I had recently purchased, while Betty was in the restroom, Dad made a degrading comment to me. "Every time I make love to Betty I think of your mother," he said quietly. I told him I couldn't believe he would say something like that to me. And then, in the next breath, he told me it would be nice if I wrote to Betty because she needed a friend. Even more shocking was the fact that Dad later told Mom that he had never had sex with Betty. Another lie!

Joe made the decision right then and there that Dad was not welcome in our home. I knew his decision was the right one. Until Dad changed, he could not be part of our lives.

During the past couple years, I have sent him many cards and letters, and he has called me a couple of times. But as soon as I hear his voice, that fidgety feeling returns and my heart starts to pound. I make an attempt to converse, but it is extremely awkward and strained. We have little in common, so it is difficult to talk for more than a few minutes.

I still experience overwhelming sadness from time to time—for the loss of mine and my sister's childhoods, for the loss of a father in my life, for my brothers, for Mom, for my children, and most of all, deep, stirring anguish for the innocent children that Dad hurt. Most perpetrators have many victims, and I suspect Dad molested children we don't even know about. And although I cannot explain why, I still feel empathy for him. It must be horrible to live with all that guilt, far, far away from the family that loves you.

All I ever wanted was a Dad who would protect me, tuck me into bed and pray with me, love me unconditionally, praise me for my accomplishments, be a fair disciplinarian, and most of all, treat my mom with respect and love God. He didn't have to be perfect or make a lot of money. I would have been content just to have him hold me without pressing against my breasts. And I know my brothers would have been delighted just to be his companion and friend.

As in the story that follows, I was a little girl with pigtails and skinned-up knees, and I wish with all my of heart that I could have climbed onto my daddy's lap and felt the warm touch of his hands wiping away my tears.

Running for Daddy![2]

by Kay Arthur

When I was a little girl—just a skinny little beanpole with pigtails—I used to run to my daddy for comfort. I was a tomboy who consistently fell out of trees, got into fights, and crashed my bicycle. It seemed like I was forever bloodying those poor, banged-up knees of mine. That's when I would run—with pigtails flying and dirty tears streaming down my face—to my daddy.

"Daddy! Daddy! Daddy!"

And I'm so fortunate, because I had a daddy who held me. Ever since I was a little girl until the day he went to be with the Lord, I was always his little sweetheart. And I would fly into his open arms, and he would gather me up on his lap—dirt, blood, and all—and hold me there. And he would wipe my tears and push back my pigtails and say, "Now, Honey, tell Daddy all about it."

Many years later I was hurting again, so very deeply.

But I couldn't run to my daddy.

I was a single mom with two little kids, trying to work and go to school. And it was one of those days when everything seemed to catch up with me— all of the hurt and loneliness and regret and pressure and weariness. I remember driving into the driveway of the little brick home where we were living. I got out of the car and began walking down the little gravel walkway toward the front door.

For some reason, time seemed to stand still for a moment.

To this day I can't tell you what triggered the thought, but suddenly—in my mind's eye—I saw something.

I saw a little girl, running.

I saw a little girl with tears streaming down her face and banged-up, bloody knees on those skinny little legs. I saw her in need of her daddy. Running for her daddy.

Then suddenly—strangely—I saw her running down a huge, shiny

corridor. A vast corridor with gleaming marble walls and beautiful windows spilling heavenly light. And at the end of that marble hallway were massive doors of brilliant gold. Standing before those doors were bright, powerful guards with great spears.

And I knew that the little girl was me, and that I was running toward the very throne room of God, sovereign ruler of the universe. Yet I was the daughter of the King of Kings, so when the guards saw me coming, they swung open those doors and let me run in. There I was, weeping and running into the very presence of God. I heard the cherubim and the seraphim crying out, "Holy, holy, holy, Lord God Almighty! Heaven and earth are full of Thy glory!" Many bowed before the throne, and court was in session, but I just ran and ran and didn't stop…

I could see Him stopping everything, opening His arms wide and just gathering me to His chest, saying, "There, there My precious child. Let Me wipe away those tears. Tell your Father all about it."

Twenty-Three

Forgiveness and Family

"We are most like beasts when we kill.
We are most like men when we judge.
We are most like God when we forgive."—Unknown

Forgiveness is a gift given to those who do not deserve it. Even more important, it is a gift to those who forgive because it frees them from bitterness, and allows them to love and pray for those whom they have forgiven. Forgiving someone who has abused you is an important step toward emotional healing. I was finally able to accept the fact that I would never have another childhood, and I knew that I wouldn't be emotionally and inwardly healed if I continued to harbor resentment and unforgiveness toward my dad. I also knew that humanly and without God's help, I could never forgive my dad. I wanted to judge my dad, but I knew I had to extend grace and mercy. I also knew that the Lord looked beyond the sin and into the sinner's childhood and heart.

It is always, always wrong to abuse a child, no matter what the circumstances. Even though Dad was sexually abused when he was a child, it didn't justify the things he did as an adult. He still had to be accountable for his sins.

In Dad's letters (unedited) dated April 7, 1999 and May 9, 2000, he shares the following words: *"Man, I sure have a king size screw loose in my head to mess up my little family and Gram and Jody and Tammy like I did. The earliest time I can remember about me being molested was when I was between the ages of 7 to 11. One of the church elders where we all went. A well respected man and a very good friend of the family, everyone in the church loved him including me. I remember him asking my parents if he could take me to the church campgrounds. He had a trailer. My mom and Dad thought this would be good for me. So off we went to camp. I slept with*

140

him and at night he would molest me over and over again. Then after two or three years I told my brother Paul and he told my mother. I remember my dad was going to kill him. After that I can't remember much of him, but from that time on I looked at girls and had a great obsession to them, and this would come over me and take complete control of my mind."

In addition to being molested by a respected church elder, several of Dad's relatives sexually molested him when he was a teenager. As I got older and became more acquainted with these relatives, I always felt uneasy and uncomfortable around them but never knew why.

I knew what the Bible said about forgiveness: *Ephesians 4:32: "And be ye kind one to another, tenderhearted, forgiving one another, even as God for Christ's sake hath forgiven you."* And *Mark 11:26: "But if ye do not forgive, neither will your Father which is in heaven forgive your trespasses."*

With God's help and a tremendous amount of faith, I have forgiven my dad. Although it will take a long time for the scars to go away completely, they are diminishing. As my pastor stated recently in a Sunday morning sermon, I am no longer the victim, but the victor.

Being part of a big family definitely has its ups and downs. Agreeing on everything all the time will never happen, but even when we disagree we still have the assurance that we are part of a special, unique family and that we love each other very much. And although many miles separate us, we remain close in heart. At the annual family Christmas Party last year, I was reminded once again just how precious each member of my family is to me.

I praise God that we were able to break the chain of abuse in our family, for the safety of others and for the safety of our own children. *Proverbs 20:7* says: *"The just man walketh in integrity: his children are blessed after him."* Every one of my siblings and their spouses are born-again Christians and leaders in their churches, and they are all wonderful parents with homes where love and integrity abide.

The unedited family testimonies and letters on the next few pages represent happy and sad times. More importantly, they represent God's faithfulness, mercy, and unconditional love.

Letter to Brothers and Sisters

I am sending all of my brothers and sisters this letter and evaluation. Not Dad. This letter to Dad was an exercise my counselor asked me to do but never to mail it to Dad. Read the letter to Dad first, then Marlene's evaluation of me after 4 months of counseling. I'm ashamed, embarrassed, and hurt. I never wanted to be like Dad, yet I was getting more and more like him every year. Remember this, though. I was stuck by his side from a child, thinking the sun rose and set on him and Uncle Stub. It's no wonder I'm most like him than the rest of us.

I feel that I have pretty much been an open book to all my family, and even though this may hurt me some by allowing you to read this letter and evaluation, that's ok. As much as I have hurt the last 4 months, a little more won't kill me. I am really sending this to all of you as a warning. Do not allow your marriage to go on year after year without regularly taking an inventory of your marriage and goals, as we have not done, or you too one day will be standing at the threshold of a rude awakening as we are. Stop taking each other for granted. Spend money and time on each other as an investment in your marriage and future and most of all, you must put God first in your marriage. Bump, Jeff, Tim, Mark, and Joe—if we're not going to put God first in our personal lives and be the spiritual leaders of our families, then do we deserve a good wife, let alone a submissive wife?

Men live by, "If it ain't broke, don't fix it." But I'm here to tell you about "Preventative Maintenance." Oil your marriage, lubricate it, repair it or align it, but whatever you do, don't wait until it's broke. Start now if you're not already doing so. You do not want to be where our marriage is today. We thought we had a good marriage—little did we know we didn't have a perfect one. We now realize that there is no perfect marriage. You just have to keep working on it like any other friendship. Let our circumstances be a warning to all of you.

Guys, learn better to communicate. Shut your mouth and just listen when your wife is trying to talk to you. Learn to be a good listener; sometimes

that's all she wants. Work on trying to understand her emotions and what makes her tick. Learn how to keep each others "Love Tank" full so they are not running on empty. Also, we need to learn how to be close and intimate. I know these can be tough things to learn, but it can be done. Whoever said "You can't teach an old dog new tricks," was wrong. I am learning daily.

Would all of you promise me that you will purchase the book *The Five Love Languages*[3], by Dr. Gary Chapman? I bought this for Matt and Katrina— perhaps their best wedding present of all, although they certainly won't realize it at this point. Read it, highlight in it, study it, and read it again as I have done. One friend of mine has read it 5 times. Learn this book and practice what it says, all of you.

I am reading the Bible daily and everything else I can get my hands on that is good or edifying. I just spotted 2 more books in a *Focus on the Family* magazine that I may order soon. As a matter of fact, this magazine shows marriage seminars all around the country. This really seems like a good idea for us. My goals are to attend perhaps the one coming up in March in Orlando, Florida, the Lord willing.

I am a changing man, father, and husband. Now that I positively realize that I was following in our dad's footsteps, I will no longer continue to do so. What a shame. Oh what wasted years!

My goal today is to draw closer to the Lord, and I am. Isn't it a pitiful shame that after a lifetime of attending First Assembly and two years of Bible school that I am at this point in my life. I know God has allowed this to happen and yes, He's got my undivided attention. Finally! Understand though, the devil has come into our marriage; God has just allowed it to happen. Notice I didn't capitalize devil!

I have learned more in the last 4 months about myself, my wife, our marriage, the Bible, and God than I have my whole life, and not because I haven't had the opportunities. Embarrassing? Yes it is!

All I can say today is "Thank you Lord for this devastating trial." Believe it or not, I even thank my precious wife, for without God and my wife, I wouldn't be where I am today. So much good is coming out of this for me and certainly for my wife too. I want all of you to know that I share in fault equally with Lori. I am praying daily for Lori and our marriage. You need to know this—that I love my wife with all that is within me. I love her more each week. I long to be with her and to be by her side. I long to have the marriage God intended us to have.

Wherever forgiveness needed to be, I have long forgiven her. That's another

thing we can thank Dad for—he did teach us the importance of forgiveness.

I pray the Lord will "fix" us both and revive our marriage to new heights and depths that we could never imagine. I know it is possible, and God can do it not only in our marriage but also in yours.

Remember, men are from Mars, and women are from Venus. We are different. Quit trying to change each other. Love your spouse as Christ loved the Church, and for who they are. Always encourage them to be the best they can be in whatever they tackle in life. We all need to learn who we really are, and with God's help to be that person whom He made us to be, our own individual, always striving to line our lives up with His plan.

"Seek ye first the Kingdom of God and His righteousness, and all these things will be added unto you." Matthew 6:33 This today is my prayer, and I am claiming His Word and truths and promises. Press on toward the mark!! Remember us in prayer, and don't forget our children.

With Love, Your Brother Mike
November 1997

Letter to Dad

Dad,

Since problems have surfaced in my marriage, I have taken a close look at myself. Sorry to say I'm not too happy in what I see. I'm learning now that I have been an incomplete husband and somewhat of a dysfunctional Father.

I know now that I have tried to manipulate my wife and others, thus having too much control over her than was healthy for a well-rounded marriage. Also, my anger (temper) and then the verbal abuse that certainly followed. I'm so sorry! I have not had the good marriage I thought I had. I have cheated my wife (I now know) in many ways, and I have taken her for granted but didn't mean to.

We have been living in "hell" for 5 weeks now, with almost no physical contact. I'm going crazy! I've lost weight. My tempter has only gripped me a couple times. My pride is gone. You and I have had too much of that anyway. I feel all alone and many times I find myself feeling sorry for me.

The good news is that I have dug into the Lord. I'm rock bottom now, and I have nowhere else to turn to go but up. I know the Lord now has me, finally, right where He wants me. I bought a new Bible, the Quest Study Bible, and I love it. I now can't wait to get up early and read it and highlight in it. The Bible has never spoken to me before like it is now. When I read a verse and think how it fits for someone else, the Holy Spirit pierces and pricks my heart and mind, and all I can do is cry and say, "Yes Lord." The Lord is chastising me so much now and remolding me into who I should have allowed Him to ever since Bible school.

I'm reading and studying everything I can get my hands on, and sometimes twice. The two books so far are *Silent Sons* and *The Five Love Languages*. Wow—what incredible books. Every newly married couple should be given *The Five Love Languages*, by Dr. Gary Chapman. Read it and practice what's in it. What a difference it would have made in my marriage.

This brings me to the purpose of my letter. I have learned so much about

who I am and what is making me tick and why I am who I am. I realize now that it all stems from my childhood and upbringing. I know that's a heavy statement, but it's so true.

I now am trying to go back into my short childhood and recall my experiences, good and bad. So, let me begin:

I don't remember much until about 4-1/2 years old, growing up in the upstairs apartment on Catalpa. By the way, that house still stands. I remember Bumpy and I playing early in the morning under the Christmas tree with our new trucks and fire truck. This is a good memory. At 5 years old, we moved to 522 Pipestone. At that time, I had to switch kindergarten schools from Columbus to Calvin Britain. Oh well, no big deal.

As you know, while I was growing up I stuck by your side like glue. I thought the sun rose and set on you. I talk about this later.

I guess my upbringing with you as my father goes something like this: Maybe you ought to sit down Dad. I'm now already crying. As far as I was concerned, you were an alcoholic, a workaholic, mean tempered, and verbally, emotionally, and sexually abusive. Some of these things I didn't realize until much later of course. I see myself on a very regular basis getting beat with your belt with my pants and underpants down to my feet. You would hold both of my wrists and whip me with the other hand as you did many times to the other boys also. Our legs and butts would be so welted and bruised that sometimes we could squeeze blood from them. You beat us way too hard. Often the neighbor kids knew from the yelling. Of course, you did always remind us that it hurt you more than it hurt us. But today, I do not believe that was a true statement. I've said it to my son, and after 3 spankings with the belt with pants down, I stopped. Before the 4th spanking, Shane and I sat down in the basement and prayed together. He was trembling as was I. The Lord told me never to spank him like that again, and I haven't. That was probably 4 years ago. He's 15 now. What a relief to rid myself of that burden.

I remember coming home from a late Tigers' baseball game. While walking home from Union Field, you drove up and yelled and said, "Get home." That night you sent me to bed with no supper (however Jody did sneak food up to me). You said, "No more ball! Quit the team!" I didn't even do anything wrong Dad, and I cried and cried. Many times we got beat before you even asked questions, later finding out the truth. Do you remember what you would say? I do. "That's for all the times you were bad and I didn't catch you." Well, that didn't make the pain of the beating go away. Certainly many times we deserved a punishment, but between your alcohol and temper, we received

more than a punishment. Mom would hurt and cry, because she knew that she could do nothing about it. She was scared too. It's no wonder she had a nervous breakdown when I was in junior high school.

Remember us usually managing to bring at least one D home on my report card. Hell usually broke loose when this happened. Whipped, grounded, verbally abused, and often made to do the dishes (for 8 people) until the next report card—usually 6 to 8 weeks. Dad, you were way too hard. It's no wonder I have shied away from dishes in my marriage. Not now though. I seem to enjoy them, and besides, it helps my wife.

You were a great "guilt tripper." You and I would be working out back on another car, and Mom and the kids would be getting ready to go to the beach. You would say, "Are you gonna sell me out and go with them or are you gonna stay and help your ol' dad?" I wasn't going to let my dad down. I look back and see myself as a child slave laborer. Before we could play, we always had to do this or that or sand and mask the next car. Of course, Bump and I did get $2.00 per car. But work always came before my childhood. At 14 years old I worked full-time in the business in the summer like a man. I know you can't argue that. The Malleable had to sign a release just to allow me to work on the roofs and slag. I carried, wheel barrowed, and roofed almost as hard and well as the men, and that's how I have worked, as you know, my whole life, the work of 2 men, much like you, Dad. Although now I realize that my workaholism has come between me and my family, I don't like it. You taught us that if we didn't work, we weren't worth our salt. Tim and I were much like you. Jeff and Bump weren't. The trouble was that you made it too well known that Jeff and Bump never seemed to meet your approval. They weren't enough like you.

You would encourage us on one hand and then knock us down and hurt us on the other hand. If what we wanted to do was not "neat" in your eyes or not manly, you would sure let us know. We were not all born to be just like you.

When I enrolled myself in singing lessons, you started making fun of me. Eventually, you got Bumpy in on the laughter, and after 3 lessons, I quit. I thought that the singing lessons were stupid too. Little did I know they were not stupid, and you were wrong again. Growing up with you, I learned a lot of how I did not want to be.

Isn't it a miracle that none of us 6 kids ever took up drinking? We saw the results of your drinking: coming home drunk and mean tempered, throwing up before you could reach the bathroom, spending all your money and checks, fighting and getting beat up—that was not what any of us wanted to be like.

So, I learned again not what to become.

I ran the roofing business as a young teenager. When something went wrong, the other men didn't get yelled at, I did. It was all my fault. One summer I didn't get paid. You said you didn't have enough money to pay me after paying the other men—and that was ok with me. But remember what you promised? That when you made it, you would buy me the car of my choice. Well, that didn't happen either. As a kid, I waited with our poles and tackle box many times on the back steps, as you had promised to take me fishing. Mom would look out at me with a broken heart, knowing you wouldn't keep your word. I was let down so much, and I really didn't understand why. I know now that you could have paid me something that summer, but you squandered your money and drank it all up. I still often wonder what really happened to the $4,000 you said we lost when you ordered that steel building.

As an adult, I know now that you lied, cheated, and stole in many ways from us. You messed with women and flirted at the bars, and I was so often with you. You would say, "Don't tell everything you hear or see." And, of course, I would never rat on you because I was 100% loyal to you.

Remember the time I drove you home from South Haven? I was a skinny little 15 year old and didn't even have a driver's license. You were too drunk, and I had never even driven on a highway, but I did it. I pushed you in the back seat, shut the door, and drove home.

Also at 15 years old, we almost lost our lives in Lake Michigan. The Coast Guard said that in 10 more minutes my heart would have stopped. All because of your stupid drinking!

Hey, the apple sometimes doesn't fall far from the tree does it? I still say "stupid" as you always did. I'm now trying not to say it as much. I don't think it shows much intelligence. I'm still biting my lip, as you have, along with Bump, Tammy, and Jeff. What a dumb habit. I'm praying that this habit will stop too.

You taught us to buck authority. Well, I have. After getting out from under you, I don't like anyone telling me what to do. I see that too is not healthy. It has caused me a great deal of hurt and trouble through my adult life. I don't wear seat belts or do much of anything I'm told to do unless I kinda do it my way. As of 11/4/97, the Holy Spirit pricked my conscience again on obeying the laws of the land. We never really have, remember? I'm sure as you live up north that you still are not obeying the rules and laws, and I know you still do it "your way." By the way, I am wearing my seat belt now. Besides, it's a good example for the kids, something, if you think about it, you were not.

Sorry Dad. I want to change. I do not want to become like you or follow in your footsteps any more. And by the grace of God, I am changing.

I hate to keep beating you up Dad, but my mind goes back to all the flirting and vulgar jokes and remarks you made about women and the times you watched the Turner girls across the street when they ran to Talbott's in their bikinis. You were sick. You taught us so much crap; it's no wonder I'm where I am in my marriage today.

I'm an adult now, and I can't blame you anymore, and I won't Dad, because I now am learning the answers as to who I really am and why. You've taught us lots and lots of good things, but the bad things just seem so overwhelming at this time.

We quit doing much with you and Mom after I was married, as did the other kids. You were mean and quick-tempered to Mom and hurt her constantly with your remarks, and it didn't matter where you were or who was around. As a child, I thought I could never have lived without you in my life (seems strange, doesn't it?), but as an adult, I've learned to live without you and now wonder how I will ever live one day without Mom. Funny how things change.

When I think of my childhood, I see you always mad and angry, or beating me with your belt and working or being by your side. I don't see a normal childhood or a small boy growing up in a functional home. I realize now that my childhood was stolen and robbed from me. No, I don't hate you, Dad, for any of this. I see now why I can't be much fun in my own marriage, like simple or silly things like decorating the Christmas tree. It wasn't macho I guess. I'm praying that the Lord will loosen me up now and teach me to be more like a child, even in my adult years. Last week I went with my wife to my first Halloween party dressed up. That was a little unusual for me, but it's a step in the right direction. I'm hoping we can take dancing lessons this winter. I guess I've been so conscious of doing things that seemed macho that I became not so fun in my marriage with my wife and kids.

I'm sorry for beating you up 7 years ago. I did beg you not to fight with me, and I did let you hit me 3 times first though. Ha ha! However, you did have it coming, and it probably, for me anyway, seemed long overdue. I regret it some days, and I am sorry, as you already know.

Dad, I honesty believe that I don't hate you and that I love you today. I know the air is thick when we're together, but maybe this too will pass. Pray for us that we will both learn together what makes us tick and that the Lord would have us remain together till death do us part and that the Lord will use

us in some type of ministry, helping, I believe, married couples in trouble. I love you. Gotta go for now.

#2 Son, Mike
November 5, 1997

In 1998, my siblings and I decided to write letters to each other for Christmas instead of exchanging gifts. We put all of our names into a hat and each one drew a name. My youngest brother, Timmy, drew my name. Following is his letter:

Dear Sis,

For anyone of my brothers, sisters, brother-in-laws, or sister-in-laws, writing this letter could be easy. You see, all of them have such wonderful attributes because they are all children of God. However, I was fortunate enough to receive your name. My only obstacle will be is if I have enough paper.

You are my big sister, Sis, or Sissy as most kids call their older sister, my friend, my mom, and my teacher. Gosh, there are so many things that I can write about. Growing up as a child I only remember bits and pieces about you, probably because you were 6 years older than me. But a few things come to my mind. You were always there for me. Any time you could help you were eager to. I remember at 542 Pipestone you would come into my room when I was practicing my horn and try to help me with rhythms and practicing methods. Wouldn't it have been great if I had worked then, instead of now?

I never had to set my alarm during the week, because you got up early to rat your hair. Hahahahahahaha! Way back in the Stone Age, you had your own bathroom for prep'n. It seems so long ago. How does time go so fast? I thank you for the little things that you did when our bedrooms were next to each other at 542 Pipestone. Once in a great while you would help me to organize my room. You know, to this day I remember you helping me make my bed. And if I were real fortunate, you would let me lie on your bed while you were practicing your flute. I always thought that your room was a museum. Every time I went in there it was in perfect order. You must have had photographic memory, because when you came home you knew if one of your stuffed animals were out of place. One thing I could never figure out

was how you knew it was me and not Tammy? The more I write the more I remember.

When you and Don were married I thought that my world as I knew it was coming to an end. You were moving away and I did not understand. However, I was fortunate as you blessed us all with Little Peeps. Oh how I loved my little niece. I thought that she walked on water. I remember coming to Detroit on the train to spend a week there with you. I was so excited to think that I would have her to myself. And then leaving was another world ending event. I cried all the way home and was mad at you and Don for moving away. Then Don went into the service and you were with us again at 542. Those days were some great memories with you and Dawnie in our house. Thank you for all the fun during those times.

And you know this would not be complete without thanking you for helping me during our marriage problems. It is a shame to think of what happened between our spouses and it would have been nice to have God step in and make everything ok. But everyone has his or her own will and He will not change it. Little did we know that we would be sharing more than a bathroom as were growing up. Hahahahaha! Hey Jody, you should write a book. Keen idea huh!

Now that we are older (you are still older) I look back at our lives and thank God that I have a sister like you that I could be so proud of. With all that you went through you are serving the Lord and that is more important than anything in the world. Many times you were knocked down and you picked yourself up and went again. It is often said that many things that happen even though it was not ordered by God that He would get the glory. Your life has glorified God and is and will continue to glorify Him as you continue to serve Him. It makes me proud to write these things about you.

Touch-typing brings on new meaning because as I am writing this I am also crying. Sometimes I miss my family so much that it hurts, yet I believe this is where God has us for now and He has given us the grace to deal without our family.

I must go now. Jody, I would like to thank you for just being you. God created you and I am happy you are my sister.

Love and kisses forever. I love you.

Testimony from My Sister, Tammy

I do not remember the exact time when my father first started molesting me. I do remember when we lived at 542 Pipestone, after my sister was gone. I would lie in bed at night and hear the stairs creak, just dreading when my dad would come into my room and start touching me. I was mortified. I felt icky. I pretended to be sleeping so that the embarrassment would not be so terrible. I mean, after all, this was my dad doing these things to me.

Sometimes I would be so afraid that I couldn't sleep, so I would take a blanket and my pillow and go sleep under my brother Tim's trundle bed. There I felt safe, and then in the morning I would quick go back to my own bed before anyone could find out. I do remember always being afraid of the dark, of the boogieman, and to this day, I cannot stay in my own home at night by myself, even though I have three children now, ages 12, 10 and 6.

I remember my father wanting to hug me and always my arms had to be above his shoulders so that he could feel my breasts against him. I remember him tickling my thighs until they hurt, and when I would tell him to stop, he would get mad and do it more. I always felt like he was looking at me, or rather, leering at me. I hated my breasts for a long time because I always thought men were looking at them and it reminded of Dad. After 15 years of marriage to a wonderful, loving husband who loves my breasts, I now love them too (ha ha).

I remember Dad yelling at my mother when we lived on the farm, and I hated him for doing that. I would tell him to stop talking to my mother that way. You see, I figured that after what he did to me, surely I had the right to see my mother treated right. Boy, was that a mistake. He would slap me (sometimes in the cheek), but I never let that stop me from sticking up for my mom.

One time, when we lived on the farm (I believe I was 21 years old), Dad had been taking some kind of medicine for what, I do not know. But apparently a side effect was that it made his penis hard for a long time. He knocked on my door (I had it locked) and begged me to open it, saying he wanted to

show me something. I was 21 years old and still I feared my dad. He must have told me that he wanted me to look at his penis, and I cannot remember if I unlocked my door and let him in or not. But after that incident, I told Mom that I wanted to be out on my own.

It wasn't long after that that my Aunt Madeline in Ann Arbor offered me a place to live, and she even said that she would help me get a job at the University of Michigan. Boy, what the Lord had in mind for me.

I had a blast living there. I did things I had never done before, like skiing, playing baseball on a league, etc. Anyway, I was going to an Assembly of God church and I met my husband there. After we started dating, I realized that I really loved him and also realized that I needed the assurance from the Lord that this was okay because I had previously prayed for a friend, and the Lord sent Mark. I thought to myself—I'm feeling more for this guy than friendship. So that is why I asked the Lord to either take away these loving feelings or show me that it was okay to love Mark in this way.

What a guy, a saint he ain't, but sometimes I still think he walks on water. When I went home to meet his folks for the first time, I knew right away they liked me, and I liked them. I finally told Mark that my father had molested me when I was young. He said it was okay, but later he told me that it scared him a little.

Boy, if he had only known, he would have probably never married me. For our life together was tons of fun in the beginning, but it was after our son, Kryn was born that I started to get sick. By sick, I guess the only way to describe it was I just could not be a wife to my husband. I couldn't let him touch me. I wanted to but I just could not, and then I would cry because I felt so bad. I figured if only Mark had married someone else who did not have all this baggage, then he would be happy. I remember planning to just leave him with the kids (our daughter Kayla was born 22 months after Kryn). I figured he would find someone else who deserved him more than me and who could be a better mother to the kids than I could.

I was plagued with terrible feelings of low self-esteem. I even thought, in the beginning of my marriage, that I did not deserve someone as wonderful as my husband, Mark. Finally, things got so bad, I begged Mark to find me a counselor and he did. I went to a psychiatrist first and only once. He was not a Christian and we realized after that one visit that he was not for me. Mark then found a wonderful Christian woman with a group in Texas called Maranatha Counseling Group (or something like that). She was the pivotal point in my getting well. I tell you, it was not easy, it took a long time, and it

is still taking a long time. I have had to deal with things like yelling at my children until they cried and then I felt so bad, I cried. I never knew I had a terrible temper until I had kids. I agonize for the time lost with Kayla. I don't remember much of her childhood or the things she did. In fact, I don't remember much of Kryn's and the details.

I do love them and I have prayed that the Lord would help me show that love to them in a better way than my own dad did. The Lord has given me wonderful friends who have joined me in prayer, and I am getting a grip on my temper. But the Lord is not finished with me yet.

I would also like to share with you another aspect of my married life that I am not proud of. I used to treat my husband terribly. Sometimes I would resent having to do things for him (like get him a cup of tea), I would ignore him, I never yelled but sometimes I said ugly things.

One day he came home from work (about four years ago) and said he did not look forward to coming home anymore. I just about died. I felt so bad, my fingertips ached all night. I prayed in bed that night and cried. I cried out to the Lord and begged him to help me be different. I told Him I needed to be different fast and I needed it to look sincere. You know you can only do things for a person for so long and be nice for so long (pretending) and pretty soon it catches up with you.

Well, guess what? I didn't have to pretend. The Lord enabled me to start treating Mark better immediately. I know that sometimes I'm still mean, but I can feel the healing process in me in that area. I love Mark more than I ever have, I want to do things more for him than I ever have, and the physical part of our marriage is the best it has ever been—and I thought things were wonderful when we were newlyweds. No comparison. I appreciate Mark more, and I truly believe that without the Lord this could not be possible. I also know that Mark, had he not been a Christian, would probably not be married to me anymore. I thank the Lord for him.

I thank the Lord for my family. We have all suffered in unspeakable ways, everyone different. But we have survived. Some of us still struggle today, and each time things come up, we have to deal with them. But guess what? We have the Lord and each other. PTL.

I am so proud of my sister for writing this book, for bringing to light all the things that have happened to her so that someone will be helped by reading this. Hopefully, someone will have their own abuse stop because of this book or will deal with what's left of their lives because of abuse. I could never have written this book. I thought about writing one once, but you see, the

Lord didn't call me to write one. He called Jody. I love her with all my heart. I only wish that we had spoken up before we did so that we could have revealed the awful things my dad was doing, but it just wasn't meant to be.

Some memories from my youth: going to the beach in the old brown truck and our friend, Jimmy Etter, hitting his head on the ceiling of the truck because Dad went over a bump by the bridge fast. We all laughed. Sitting in the living room at 522 Pipestone in front of the Christmas tree and having someone pound on the windows from outside at night. We were so scared we practically pulled each other from running up the stairs to get to where Mom was. It was one of my brothers. I also remember sitting in the stairs with somebody else, crying, while my father was upstairs beating one of my brothers. Leaning over the kitchen sink sprinkling white sugar on my buttered bread for a snack. Playing in the huge mud puddles on the side of the house and watching the mud squish up between our toes—what fun. Having popcorn and homemade fudge every Saturday night and watching Lawrence Welk and loving it. Getting Nehi pop and ice cream from the party store down on Pipestone and having bowls of ice cream with pop over them.

Some bad memories: Dad asking me to come into the bathroom to wash his back and really he wanted me to rub his penis until he ejaculated, telling me to go downstairs to the basement at 542 Pipestone and asking me to pull my pants down while he made me lean over a 50 gallon drum and he would put Vaseline on his penis and then have me stand with my legs together and he would put his penis between my upper thighs. Oh how I hated that. I hated everything he made me do. He would make me perform oral sex on him until he ejaculated. He always had a condom on.

I was saved at church camp when I was 12. One day, after that, in the bathroom, he said he wanted to show me how babies were made. I asked him if that was a sin, and he said yes. I said, then I don't want to do it. The active part of the incest stopped at that time. No more trips to the bathroom or the basement or up to my room, but the looks, hugs, and tickling continued until I left the house when I turned 21.

Love, Tammy
1999

Testimonies from My Daughter, Dawn

I always knew that my mother and her siblings didn't have the best father in the world when they were growing up. I had heard stories about his drinking and various forms of cruel punishment. I had always assumed that he was healed from that because I never witnessed any of the bad stuff while I was growing up. I guess I just figured that those days were long gone and he was fine now. In my young mind, people who were once "bad" could just become "good." I really didn't give it another thought. In fact, when my parents were separated, my mother, brother, and I moved in with my grandparents. I remember my grandpa taking care of us, providing us with basic needs and acting as a father figure.

That all changed drastically in 1988. My grandpa molested my younger cousin. I don't know the exact chain of events, but I believe my cousin told her father, which opened up the case for police involvement. My grandpa was eventually arrested and convicted, although I am not sure of the final charges. My grandparents ended up getting divorced, and my grandpa moved up north. The time period in between these events shattered a family that I once believed to be as close as they could be.

I would have been 16 or 17 and just getting ready to begin my senior year of high school in Saline, Michigan. Life had been pretty good for me. I had been through my parent's divorce and your normal teenage boyfriend problems and breakups, but nothing that was earth shattering. I cannot remember the exact time and place when I was told what had happened in my family, but I do remember feeling disbelief. I believed that what my mother was telling me was true, however, it was difficult for my thought processes to fully take in and comprehend the information.

As the details started coming out, I learned that my grandfather had molested my mother and her sister, my aunt, many times while they were growing up. I never had any idea that this had happened to them. My mother had never mentioned this to me. I wasn't sure if this was because she had repressed this or if it was because she just wasn't ready to share this with me.

I remember feeling hurt and sad for those he molested and my grandmother for what she would now have to deal with. My grandparents had just built a new log cabin home in their hometown, which was a dream for my grandma. I remember wondering what would happen to their home and if they would divorce and how sad it would be for them.

This was time of soul searching for me. I remember having such conflicting feelings about my grandpa. Of course my allegiance was to my mother, aunt, cousin, and grandma. But this was my grandpa. The one who had called me 'Lil Peeps since the day I was born. The one who took me to the Red & White grain store for animal food all the time. The one who always let me pick out a present at the checkout counter. This was the one who took care of my mom and brother and me when my parents separated. It was very hard for me to detach myself from him emotionally. I didn't want to have a relationship with him anymore because he did such horrible things. However, I was sorry and sad for him and just couldn't be mean to him or quit talking to him when he called. I had such conflicting emotions.

I really felt badly for my mom. I couldn't believe that she could carry such a burden around for so many years without telling us. I didn't know if she had gotten help or if she even needed help or what I could do for her. She had remarried a wonderful man in 1987, and he took good care of us all. For this I was grateful. I knew I could count on my new stepfather to take care of her and listen to her and support her while this was going on.

I felt badly for my grandmother also. My grandfather and her had what I thought to be a good marriage. It was very traditional: 6 kids, numerous grandchildren, Christmas holidays with the family at the house, birthday celebrations, etc. I can remember my grandma and grandpa dancing around the living room at times when there was a good song on the radio. It was a comfortable life. Now that would all be gone. I don't know if she initially knew she was going to divorce him or if that decision came later. It must have been such a hard time for her. I remember how hard it was when I broke up with a boyfriend after dating him for only a couple months—this was a man she had been with for decades and had a family with. My grandmother is such a cute, sweet, wonderful person. I couldn't imagine anyone doing her wrong!

I felt badly for my aunt and cousin. My cousin was so young, only 8. Her life was just beginning, and now to have to deal with this. I knew this would affect her for the rest of her life. I felt glad that I was never molested by my grandpa, but I felt a little guilty too. Why them and not me? I had gone with

him on over-night trucking trips and nothing ever happened.

I had two sets of relationships that were supposed to be role models my grandparents and my parents. Both relationships had turned out to be nothing to look up to (not to any fault of my grandmother or mother). I only had these dysfunctional marriages and men to look up to. I believe that this played a part to my choosing the wrong man to marry when I was 23 years old.

My family is surviving this tragedy. My grandmother had to sell her cabin. She purchased an adorable ranch home in a small country subdivision. It is the coziest home I've ever been in. I love spending weekends with her, although they are few and far between due to my work schedule. I know that my grandmother talks to my grandpa from time to time. She seems to be happy. She has a lot of faith in God, which I'm sure will help her be a survivor.

My mother has a wonderful marriage to a man who loves God very much. I know that he loves her and has helped her get through this, and she is now sharing her experience with other survivors.

I am deeply saddened by what my family had to go through. However, I work for a police department and hear stories every day that are much worse than what my family went through. I am not trying to belittle this tragedy in any way. It just helps me to realize that there are people living in this world who have experienced things much worse than I could ever imagine. There is always someone whose story is more tragic. My family is all alive and healthy.

I can speak for myself and say that I am happy and content with life. Although I have been through some tough times, I am not bitter. I know now (although I didn't always realize this) that there are men out there who will treat their wives good and be responsible husbands. I am currently in a relationship with a man who loves me very much and shows it and says it on a consistent basis. Together we are trying to build a good life. We have found a church that we enjoy, and that we are very involved in. We communicate freely. I can tell him/ask him anything and I know I will get an honest answer. I still have moments of insecurity, and I can be very emotional at times. I think these traits, especially the insecurity, derive in part from the breakup of my parents, grandparents, and my own marriage. However, it hasn't made me incapable of forming a solid relationship.

I am glad that my mother is able to tell other women about her experience. I know that those women will be touched and helped by her testimony. That is only a small reward though for what she had to endure. However, maybe she is all some women will have. Maybe they don't have a family that is

open and that they can discuss their problems with. I am proud of my mother. She was and continues to be a good mother. She has always been fair and just and she is a good role model. She has turned a horrible experience into a "what can I do for someone else now" situation. I love my mother very much.

Dawn
1998

As a person who has suffered some tragedy in my lifetime, I have also been blessed beyond belief. When I step back and take a look at the broad picture of my family, I can see that they have all been hurt by what my grandfather did. I also see aunts, uncles, cousins, a mother, grandmother, and more who are just trying to make it through life and deal with what has happened to them. I am proud of each and every one of my family members because they all have something to offer this world. I see a family who is trying hard to serve God and do the right things. While no one in my family is perfect, (including me), they all really try to be the best they can. Surely there will be mistakes made along the way.

However, if there is one thing I have learned it is this: If you make God the primary go-to-person in your life, you will be rewarded. Without faith, it is difficult, and even impossible to make it through trials and tragedies. And life will bring them!

I am thankful that my parents laid down a Christian foundation for me to draw upon. After all that has happened in my life, I just wanted God to send me a husband who could truly be a friend and supporter. I wanted a husband who was as into being a husband as I was into being a wife. I wanted to know that my faith in relationships was not too badly damaged. I was blessed with exactly that person in Todd Pickett. We were married in August of 1998 after dating for almost two years. Our marriage is exactly what I always thought a marriage should be.

I keep a lot of my relationship with God quiet and personal. However, I pray for my family all the time. I pray for every aunt, uncle, cousin, grandparent, mother and stepmother, father and stepfather, brother, and in-laws. I pray that God can continue to work in their lives and continue to heal the hurts that have been caused. And the best thing is that I know HE will.

Dawn
2000

Testimony from My Mother, Barbara

My kids were bus kids (called Pixies by the other kids). In 1958 I was visiting a friend in the project on McCord Street when she mentioned to me that she sent her children to Sunday school on a school bus. How wonderful, I thought. I'll drive my children to her house and send them with hers. But, the next Sunday when I drove them over to the project and started to put them on the bus, the bus driver greeted me by name, and it turns out that he knew me. It was Chuck Magner. He offered to pick my children up right at my own home and take them to Fair Plain Assembly of God on Cherry Street in Benton Harbor, Michigan.

After my husband got saved at the Assembly of God Church on Highland Avenue in December of 1959, we switched and started going as a family to that church (now First Assembly). All six of my children were dedicated in that church. As my two oldest, John (Bump) and Jody started playing instruments, David Will, Albert Liedtke, Tim and one of the Juengling boys took them under their wing and encouraged them to play in the church orchestra. In 1962, the church moved to First Assembly on Nickerson Avenue. There each of my six children were saved and baptized. They were very active in Christian Cadets, Royal Rangers, Missionettes, Orchestra, Choir, and Waylighters, and they attended the summer camp in Bridgeman, Michigan every year. Five of my six children were also married in this church. Performing the ceremonies were Rev. Alvin Sprecher, Rev. Wally Riehl, and Rev. Raymond Rueb.

Now, 40 years later, my six children, Bump (John), Jody, Mike, Jeff, Tim, and Tammy are still serving the Lord. They and their spouses and children are involved in choir, orchestra, special music, Sunday school, youth groups of various kinds, and worship teams.

Praise the Lord for that bus being there that Sunday morning. Who knows where we all would be had it not been for the bus ministry. We thank the Lord for protecting us, guiding us, loving us, and saving us for His Kingdom, and for directing us to the First Assembly of God in the first place.

To God be the Glory for the things He hath done.

Barbara
March 2000

Testimony from My Youngest Brother, Timmy

I printed your book off yesterday and read the entire book. I have to tell you that my emotions are all over the place. Again I have to sort out my feelings about Dad: from rage to hate to despise to hurt to dismay, you name it. How and why I still love him is a puzzling thought. I asked the Lord this morning, "how come you let it happen"? I know that it wasn't His plan; however, I just hurt over the entire thing. You know what I mean. At any rate, this will give me another opportunity to get closer to the Lord.

I am so sorry that this happened to you, Tam, our niece and the other little girl. Innocence turned into troubled lives. My heart is broken again. God will help me Jod. This is just reality.

I support you and Joe with all my prayers and all my being. I will help you to carry the word that God has given you in any way called upon by you or God. Count me in to fight this terrible war to save the innocence of our children. My Love for you is great and I can only hope that in God's way He will turn this tragedy into Glory for Him. I love you and I am soooooooooooooo proud of you that I could burst. It takes insurmountable courage to carry this cross. You will need a lot of prayers to go with you, and I will be one that will support you in prayer.

All my Love, Timmy
September, 2001

Letter from Uncle Ken

Jody and Tammy,

It seems appropriate for me to write this letter to both of you since you both went through the sexual abuse as young girls by your father.

Aunt Karen and I have always loved you girls as our own. We have sat in church many times over the years with tears in our eyes as we watched you serve the Lord with your musical talent.

I believe Jody's manuscript is not only well done, but a story that I am so grateful she put into print. Sin hidden is sin never conquered. Jody has revealed the truth of your father's violence and sin.

Every time I think of how my brother neglected your family, denied his wife the sacredness of the marriage vow physically and sexually, and abused his children, I can only say, "unbelievable!" I cannot understand how any father could abuse an innocent child that he is called to protect. It is beyond my imagination.

I am so happy that the Lord doesn't look at where we've been or what we've been through, but where we are headed and where we are now.

I appreciate the fine lives you girls are living and am so happy you have Godly husbands to love and be loved by. I am so grateful that you have been blessed with fine children whom you can love and be loved by and that you can protect one another.

As I have visited your father in prison over the past few years, I always ask, "How could you have hurt your beautiful daughters?" He has no answers, shows no remorse, claims Christ, but still doesn't seem to realize the damager he has inflicted and seems void of the understanding of true repentance.

My greatest fear is that some day he may leave the prison gates and reenter the lives of your mom, you girls and your brothers. If he is ever released it will only be a short time before he will recommit these same (or other) crimes against innocent children.

I don't know if I have forgiven your father, but with the Lord's help I am

trying and know and believe the scriptures about forgiving those who have offended. I know you are taught to honor your father and am convinced that the Lord will honor our efforts to forgive. My only hope is that you will do it from a distance, never putting yourselves at risk of more mental abuse.

Through this period of years, I trust you have learned to love your husbands, children, and family even more. It is a wonderful thing to love and be loved by a spouse. I trust you are helping your husbands become the best men they can possibly be. In return, you will realize you are becoming the best persons, wives, mothers, daughters, sisters, aunts (and nieces) that you ever thought possible.

The Lord brings you to my mind often, and I thank Him for the fine nieces you are! I love you both very much and trust for God's best for you and those you love.

Uncle Ken
June 13, 2002

Twenty-Four

Prison

One of the things I remember most about Dad is the verbal abuse and yelling. When Dad was in the house, we walked on thin ice so we wouldn't provoke him. He talked to Mom like she was a filthy dog, and it made me so mad that I could barely contain my anger. Even at the risk of getting slapped, I coldly and aggressively stood up to him and told him that he shouldn't talk to her that way. My spitefulness and lack of fear only compounded his anger. Mom was scared to death every time I tried to defend her, because she knew Dad was capable of inflicting serious injury on me. I didn't care. I wasn't afraid.

Tammy felt the same, often telling Dad not to talk to Mom that way. Then Dad would slap her or yell at her.

When my daughter was young, there were many times when I lost my temper and screamed at her so viciously that the veins in my neck almost penetrated my skin. The physical and verbal abuse I inflicted on her was very damaging. The memories of those times are so disturbing that I have asked the Lord to remove them from my mind forever. If I close my eyes, I can envision my precious little girl cowering in the corner of her bedroom while I lashed out at her. The time the belt slipped out of my hand and the buckle cut her leg while I was whipping her is especially agonizing. Children should be accountable to those in authority over them, but no child should ever be subjected to something or someone so out of control.

I did not know it then, but I know now that I was acting out the physical and verbal abuse I lived in as a child. I grew up in a home where my dad's vicious yelling and temper was commonplace. Still, there was no excuse for my behavior. I had a choice. I made the wrong one.

As a child, I was trapped in an abusive, dysfunctional home and exposed to sex at a very vulnerable age by the person I loved and trusted most—at an age when my only care should have been how to dress my dolls. I trusted my

dad, and he betrayed me over and over and over again. The exposure to sex at such an innocent, tender age magnified my need for touch and warped my comprehension and understanding of true, pure love. And Dad's rigid control over me while I was growing up caused a desperate need in me to control everything and everyone in my own life.

After the separation from my first husband, there was a time when I lived in repulsive sin, having sexual relationships with several men to whom I was not married. During these encounters, I was in control and once again soaring high above anyone and anything that could hurt me. Only this time, instead of on a swing as an innocent child, I was in bed with another man as a grown adult. When I wasn't having sex, I was fantasizing about it. The lustful thoughts and need to be held literally controlled my every action and thought.

I would leave my apartment late at night after my children were asleep and return in the dark, early morning hours so that no one would see me— something I had learned from my dad, the master of deception. Once, when I walked in the back door of my apartment after one of these encounters, I found Matthew sitting in the kitchen with his head resting on the table. He had been worried about me and had fallen asleep while waiting for me to come home. The guilt nearly killed me, but it touched my heart forever.

I thought that my emptiness, loneliness, and low self-esteem could only be fulfilled in the arms of men. In a desperate attempt to find acceptance and love in the only way I knew how, I gave myself away physically. But instead of freeing myself from my past, I was plunging my life deeper and deeper into enslavement, and my heart was becoming more and more calloused. I tried to convince myself that my sin was justified. Although it is agonizing to admit these things about myself, I no longer feel guilt and shame because I know that I have been forgiven.

For years I suffered from addictive behaviors caused by my abuse: sadness, worry, perfectionism, lust, and a detailed, unsettled mind.

I am still an obsessive perfectionist—a lower standard is not an option. If I see one crumb on my kitchen counter or floor, I can't just remove the one crumb, I have to clean the entire counter and floor. My underclothing, socks, and nylons are arranged by color and style in perfect piles in my dresser drawers. My blouses, dresses, slacks, and suits are organized in my closet by color, short and long sleeves, and length. My shoes—well, that's another story! Correspondence and working files on my desk at home and work are placed so that they line up flawlessly with the side of the desk—if they accidentally get shuffled, I instantly become agitated. Being a perfectionist

can become an idol if you allow it to control you. The Lord is still healing me in this area.

Most of my life, I suffered with serious constipation that often resulted in impacted bowels and bleeding. One time after delivering a bowel the size of an aerosol can, a huge hemorrhoid popped out of my rectum and the blood began to drip into the toilet. I screamed for Joe, and when he saw the size of what was in the toilet, he immediately called my physician's assistant. Within an hour I was having surgery to remove this hemorrhoid.

I am thankful that I was referred to incredible gastro specialists at Chapel Hill University Medical Center in North Carolina, where I was diagnosed with colonic inertia and pelvic floor dyssynergia, the result of holding my bowels in for days at a time. One of the effects of my childhood sexual abuse was that my colon and intestines didn't know how to operate properly. At that time, the specialists at Chapel Hill University discussed the possibility of doing an ileostomy on me—this is when they close your rectum and give you a colostomy bag. The thought of it nearly paralyzed me. This is when I agreed to participate in a six-month biofeedback study to retrain my sphincter muscles to relax and push the right way when I have a bowel movement. Although the therapy sessions were embarrassing and sometimes wearisome, they were critical to my future health. Now, I am happy to say that I have a normal bowel movement nearly every morning, something that many people take for granted. As I put into practice what I have learned, I am confident that my physicians and God will heal me totally.

I still struggle with immense sadness and lustful thoughts. I still grieve, especially on Father's Day. And the fear of being pregnant with my dad's baby at age 13 left an emotional scar that may never completely go away.

Dad made my siblings and me accountable to rules to which he himself did not abide. "Do as I say, not as I do," was his motto. All my life, especially during my career as an executive secretary and my participation in a large church orchestra several years ago, those in authority over me told me to be an example and raise the standards by being accountable to a different set of rules than the other employees and musicians. In the corporate environment, I felt it was the worst possible form of management. My philosophy is to discipline those who were breaking the rules and reward those who were abiding by them. In the church, the music director concealed the bad attitudes and lack of respect of many musicians by extending grace over and over again, only because he was afraid of confrontation and because he needed their instruments in the orchestra. Covering up the wrongdoing didn't

accomplish anything positive and it certainly didn't help those who were sinning—instead, it caused hurt feelings and spread bad morale among the other musicians. Being the scapegoat infuriated me then and infuriates me now. When I am exposed to lack of accountability in others, I have to immediately put my invisible blinders on and remind myself that I am only responsible for my own actions and that I cannot change others.

All of my siblings have been grossly affected by the abuse they were subjected to as children. One of my brothers wet his bed nearly every night until he was almost 20 years old—he didn't have a physical problem—he had no self-worth because Dad mocked and rejected him. Another brother is still a workaholic, something he learned from Dad. Another sibling is still controlling.

Mom suffered inexpressible trauma, because she not only grieved for herself, she grieved for each of her six children and her grandchildren. In addition, she felt the pangs of guilt at not knowing that her daughters were being sexually molested. All of the "what ifs" played over and over in her mind like a broken record. Although I am sure many will question her unawareness, there is no doubt in mine and my family's minds that she is innocent of any wrongdoing. Mom's counselor from St. Joseph, Michigan, Gloria Gillespie, offered the following comment on behalf on my mother: "Nine out of ten mothers know about their children's abuse, but there is always an exception. Your mother could very well be that exception—the tenth mother."

What drives a man to maliciously beat and rape his children? I will never know. He may never know. The experts may never know. The fact that Dad and Mom had sex almost every night of their married lives tells me that Dad's addiction to pornography and sex could not be blamed on any lack. It is my opinion that his addiction was an emotional and mental disease that held him in such inconceivable bondage that he was never strong enough to break free. And yet, he had a choice.

Dad never recovered from his own childhood abuse and trauma—there was no one to show him the way. His heart was enslaved by sexual lust, and in a lascivious attempt to fill his own emotional needs, he abused his family. Still, he had a choice.

By making him accountable to God and to the laws of our land, we showed him compassion and love. Courage—it took so much courage!

In March 1999, Dad sexually molested another child—an eight-year-old neighbor girl who grew up knowing and loving him like a grandfather. He

was convicted of CSC (Child Sexual Conduct) and sentenced to 7 to 20 years in prison without parole.

When the letter came from my brother with the news, my reaction was shock, incredible and immense shock. As my husband spilled out the unbelievable words while driving me home from work one evening, it was as if a sharp knife had sliced away another piece of my heart. Joe tried to calm me down. "Breath slowly, honey, breath slowly. You're going to be okay. You're safe." Again, my family and I experienced overwhelming grief for Dad, but most of all, for the innocent child. Although we agreed with the court's decision and knew he had to go to prison, knowing that he would probably die behind bars was shattering. Mike made a heartfelt attempt to break the news to us as gently as he possibly could in the following (unedited) letter dated March 12, 1999:

Regretfully, I write this letter to all of you and with much sorrow and sadness. Dad has committed CSC second degree again with the neighbor girl up north (8 years old) in early November. She grew up knowing and loving Dad as a grandfather. Her parents loved Dad as a father.

About two months ago, Dad called me and said he needed me to come up. I could tell it was urgent, so I left the next morning at 6:00 a.m. I figured this was what it was, but Lori and I were hoping for the best. My heart sank as Dad told me what happened, and I was filled with anger and disgust. But, Dad needed a friend, and you all know I could not leave him now. Dad had already made several arrangements as he was awaiting his trial and his March 9th sentencing. Well, we changed much that he had done. Dad had hoped that I would be responsible for his legal and financial affairs while he was incarcerated, but he knew he shouldn't ask. He said that he had hurt all of us enough. Well, he has, as I told him, but I still love him and I want to do what is best for him.

Dad was very relieved to hear that I would take care of his matters. He was very nervous and scared, but with spending the day up north with him and my willingness to help, Dad was relieved. Lori and I helped Dad prepare a new will, and I now have full power of attorney and medical power of attorney. His gravesite is purchased, and I have all his instructions upon his death.

Dad made good money up north but has little to show for it. He

lived and spent carelessly, big hearted, generous and helped or gave to his friends. Dad sold things so cheap (car and truck) because he thought the law would take him sooner. He gave probably $5,000 worth away. This is how he was and that's ok, I guess.

I am going to ask $20,000 for his property and may only end up with $16,000 or so—who knows. Should any of our family be interested, let me know. Dad wanted Lori and I to buy the property, but after the last few trips up here, I see for me it would be too sad to vacation in Dad's home. When the trailer does sell, Dad's estate might be worth $25 to $30 thousand dollars. Dad said it best. "Not much to show for a 70 year old man, is it?" His personal belongings are all packed in boxes. I'm not sure yet what I will do with them when the trailer sells.

As Dad said his good-byes, when we were finalizing his affairs in town, many cried and said, "we love you John." It was so tough as I cried everywhere we went. You either loved Dad or you didn't; there was no in-between.

Dad had a court appointed attorney who did a great job on Dad's behalf. He was hoping for only 5 years in prison. Awaiting sentencing, we laughed and cried; he was so glad I was there with him. I told him even though I am joking some, that inside I hurt so bad. Many times we just cried. The sentencing didn't go so well. When both attorneys were done, I just had to raise my hand. The judge called on me and for a moment all I could do was stand there and cry. I tried to talk on Dad's behalf but to no avail. The judge lashed out at me as to what did I do to prevent this from happening, then told me, "that's enough, return to your seat." Well, I could have punched him out don't you know, for being so rude. Ha ha. Dad got 7 to 20 years with no parole. So, he will probably serve 7 years from today (March 10, 1999). I believe he will be transferred to Jackson and eventually to a medium security prison.

I played a song for Dad in my truck on the way to court and told him how it ministered to me the last year or so. I will be mailing his Bible and highlighters whenever he gets situated. I told Dad this may be his last wakeup call and will he rise to the occasion and seize the moment or continue while in prison with his same frame of mind only once again to give satan the victory.

This has been a great loss to the family up north whose child Dad

molested, as they loved him. Many of us could say if we only did this or that and many of us are hurting because we wish we would have helped more, but as you know, Dad didn't want our kind of help. That would have been too hard for him; it was much easier to live the way he chose. Preaching to him doesn't help. What he does with the rest of his life is what matters. I did have some very frank conversations with him and thoughts, when I could sneak them in. The bottom line is, you are what you eat. Fill your mind with crap and trash and you become that. Dad says he's got a demon inside of him. I guess I can't argue that. Dad was not only molested by a Christian friend, but also repeatedly by his cousin whom we called Uncle Bud, and a baby sitter. At a young age, he found himself quite knowledgeable with sexual things and compounding this with the loss of his father at 11 years old, it's no wonder he has led such a life. Now, he just wants to rest in peace—what a shame and a waste. I told him that you have just pissed your whole life away and regretfully, he had to agree.

Oh, a couple of years back as Dad talked of this little girl, I asked him then, "do the parents know what happened before you moved up north?" Dad said yes, I told them everything. Well, I know now he lied to me so I called Debbie (the mother) last night and asked her. Dad only told of his long marriage to Mom and his divorce and that he was the cause, nothing else. See, Dad has made his own bed once again and he has to lie in it. I am so thankful that I and you do not. He made his own choices—not us.

Misty wrote a wonderful letter to Pops and said "I forgive you and I love you." I am so thankful for this healing in her heart and life. When I returned home from my first trip up north, Lori and I sat Shane down and told him everything, as he did not know what happened before. Shane was getting to know Dad and thought he was the best, and Shane will love Dad no matter what. I realize every one of us will have to work through this in our own way. Just remember, it takes more energy to hate, not forgive and hold a grudge, then it does to forgive and love him even with his bad points. Lori summed it up well the other night when she said, "look at all the neat things your dad has contributed to your lives, such as love, sharing, family closeness, personality, outgoingness, instruments, the Lord and church, and the list could go on and on. Perhaps when you're ready and I have an address for Dad, you too may want to write and think of some of the

good times and good things he instilled in us.

Betty (a lady that cares for and loves Dad), called me last night so worried. She would marry Dad if she could. She seemed like a very smart gal. She said you guys must have had a wonderful and extraordinary mother. Well, I would only agree, as you do too.

Listen, I wanted to tell all of you sooner (when Dad told me), but he asked me not to say a word until he was gone. I told him that I did not agree with this at all and that I feel his family should know. Well, he again asked me not to say anything to anyone and I reluctantly agreed. Hope you all understand. Dad could very well die in prison. Tonight is only his second night. I hurt for him. Please pray for him.

With Love, Your Brother Mike xo

On March 19, 2000, the *Ludington Daily News* printed the following article:

51st Circuit Court
Gets 7-22 on CSC Charge

John Adam Enders, 70, Fountain, was sentenced to 7 to 22 ½ years in a Michigan Department of Corrections institution for criminal sexual conduct, second degree, second offense, and being a habitual offender, second offense. He was given three days jail credit and ordered to pay a $150 lab fee.

A couple days later, my brother Jeff, always a source of encouragement, sent me the following note:

Hi Joe and Jody and Puppy,

Well, another bombshell. Sitting in my office late one night I opened Mike's letter and wambee! My heart is broken. We had begun to reach out to Dad—camping, hunting and such. Going to breakfast was a real challenge because of how he acted. Nonetheless, we tried. Em and Seth are crushed, with Em crying late into the night. Do pray for their tender hearts. I also will need much prayer and counsel to get through this.

My prayer for you is a renewed hope in the things of Christ. I do adore you and will pray daily for you. Mary Sue is being real good about this, with compassion towards those that hurt so badly. Oh boy! She is working with and loving up the kids and me too. Also Shane

and Misty are hurting. Bump and Nancy were stunned.

Love, Jeff

I suspected that Dad was still molesting children long before I received Mike's letter dated March 12, 1999. In January 1998 while visiting my family in Michigan, I told Mike that I knew in my heart that Dad was molesting another child. Mike knew too, but he couldn't tell me because he had made a promise to Dad and felt he had to keep his word.

In November 1999, Dawnie, Mom, and I visited Dad where he may spend the rest of his life. As we approached the brick building with the high barbed wire fences, I was already choking back the tears. For a moment, just as we began walking down the sidewalk to the front door of the formidable-looking, lonely place, I thought I would have to back out. I didn't know if I had the mental or physical strength to endure seeing Dad behind bars in a maximum-security prison. He was in lockup for 22 hours a day, allowed out of his cell only to eat his meals.

I knew Dad was waiting for me though, and I could not disappoint him. The co-dependent relationship was still prevalent.

After we removed our socks and shoes and were searched by a female guard, we were led into a large room filled with inmates and family members. Many of the inmates had earned the privilege of wearing street clothes, but I immediately spotted my dad in a royal blue prison uniform. With all my mental and emotional fortitude, I tried to be strong. But I broke down and cried so hard that I had to turn my face to the wall.

When I finally turned around, Dad was running towards me with his arms opened wide. He was the prodigal father returning to his daughter. I was the little girl longing for my daddy's embrace. For the first time in my life, he held me as a father. Over and over again he repeated the words that were so unbelievable to me, "It's so good to see you, Jod. It's so good so see you."

I have heard that sexual offenders can be helped but not cured. But I believe that God can forgive and change the vilest sinner. In *Isaiah 1:18, it says, "Come, let's talk this over, says the Lord; no matter how deep the stain of your sins, I can take it out and make you as clean as freshly fallen snow. Even if you are stained as red as crimson, I can make you white as wool!"*

I cannot talk to Dad on the telephone and cannot afford to fly to Michigan very often to see him. The only contact I have with him at this time is through writing. When I receive a letter from him, I have to rely on the Holy Spirit to

give me discernment regarding his sincerity. Since his imprisonment, I believe he has given himself back to the Lord. I know he wishes he could live his life over and have another chance at being a father. I have no doubt that he thinks about his family, probably every hour of every day, that he is proud of all of his children and grandchildren, and that he loves each one very much. In one of his letters, he said I would always be his special little gal and that he wouldn't blame me if I never wrote to him again, and even if I cut his body into ten thousand pieces, every piece would still say, "I love you, Jody."

My dad married the most wonderful woman in the world and she became my mother. He helped give me life. He provided food, clothing, and shelter for me. He sent me to Sunday school, and there I gave my heart to Jesus. He rescued my children and me when we had no place to go. For these things, I will always be grateful.

I don't know if Dad ever accepted true accountability for his sins, but I want to believe that he is truly remorseful, that he has given his heart back to God, and that he loves me. This is, and will remain, my hope....

Twenty-Five

The End, or Perhaps, the Beginning

Shortly after Dad was sent to prison, I was wrongly accused and fired from my job by a supervisor whom I thought was my friend, my mom had breast cancer, and my husband was hospitalized with kidney stones. All of this happened within a month's time. Desperation poured into my mind and soul like a monsoon. I wanted to swallow the whole bottle of sleeping pills that had been prescribed to me, but God's presence in the deepest crevices of my soul kept me from it. I was not able to emotionally withstand the traumatic effects of these multiple tragedies and had to get help. When my physician's assistant recommended an anti-depressant, my initial reaction was one of guilt and inadequacy, as though I didn't have enough faith in God. I thought that being a Christian should be enough to pull me through these tough times. Christians often forget that they are human too.

After years of coping with hurt and rejection, covering up my dad's sins, and pretending that nothing was wrong, uncontrollable anger began erupting out of me like a volcano. My family could see what was happening, and being able to openly talk about my anger helped me understand that I needed serious counseling. The psychiatrist with whom I met helped me see that my anger was justified, that it was a necessary part of my healing, and that the Lord wanted to heal the hurt that was causing the anger. But first, I had to admit to myself that I was still harboring immense anger and bitterness. It was such a relief to let the tears flow during my counseling sessions. I cried so much and so hard that I thought I would drown in my own tears.

God will use the hideous, tragic circumstances of my life because I obediently surrendered them. I could have let my hurt make me calloused. Instead, I asked God to help me use my past to make me more tender and compassionate so that I will be more sensitive to others who are hurting. More importantly, I am trying to find mercy for those who fail, including myself.

As long as we allow our painful past to keep us in bondage, we will continue to be victims. Feeling better about ourselves is an act of trust and a mental choice that we have to make at the dawn of every new day. And sometimes, in order to have a positive testimony, we have to experience and overcome some type of tragedy or opposition. After we have gone through the trial, we can then testify of the great victory of God's faithfulness and love. *Isaiah 49:16* says: *"Behold, I have indelibly imprinted (tattooed a picture of) you on the palm of each of my hands."* God knows every day of our lives, and although He doesn't cause the painful trials, He can use them for His good and ours.

As a child, I experienced anger, frustration, bitterness, unworthiness, guilt, disappointment, betrayal, hurt, and fear. As an adult, I lived through many years of uncertainty, financial insecurity, loneliness, and heart-wrenching depression and sorrow—these horrible effects of my childhood trauma often caused me to make wrong choices.

These years have been returned to me, and I have been blessed with a wonderful husband, two precious children, and a wonderful son-in-law and daughter-in-law. I am extremely proud of their accomplishments and integrity.

Joe and I have been married for almost 16 years and together have endured many triumphs and tragedies. He continues to enjoy his retirement, although he is busier than ever. He does the grocery shopping, takes care of our one-acre yard, our neighbor's yard, our dog, and all of the domestic chores, including the laundry, and he recently went back to work part time. When he occasionally drives me to work on rainy days, it is not uncommon to see him sitting near the front door of my workplace with an umbrella, waiting to escort me to the car so I wouldn't get wet. He often has delicious meals and bubble baths prepared for me when I get home from work.

I have a flute figurine collection with almost 100 figurines from all over the world, and he is always searching for additions to my collection. One evening, while browsing in a Hallmark, I found a musical instrumental angel collection. There was one missing, and I said, "Look, honey, the one that's missing must have been the one that was playing the flute." Earlier, while I was on the other side of the store looking at stationery, Joe had quickly purchased the angel, ran to the car, hid it under the seat, and returned to the store all in a couple minutes.

When we got in the car, he said, "I bought you something, honey." He knows how much I enjoy surprises, and this was no exception. He handed me the Hallmark box, and when I opened it and unfolded the tissue paper,

there was the angel playing the flute.

A couple months ago when I walked in the back door one evening, he said, "Close your eyes, honey. I have a surprise for you." As he held my hand and gently guided me into the bedroom, I tried to imagine what he had done this time. When I opened my eyes, I saw a slide projector on the bed, and on the wall, a baby picture of my daughter. Because most of my children's baby pictures are in slide form, I had not seen them for many, many years. I ran to him, threw my arms around him, and through my tears said, "This is the best surprise you have ever given me." Truly, Joe's joy comes from giving.

Many incest victims become promiscuous, are emotionally crippled, become infected with venereal diseases, are driven to alcohol or drugs, murder their abusers, or take their own lives. Not all survivors are capable of having meaningful relationships, so I know that my relationship with Joe is a miracle.

Our relationship isn't perfect. We are very different and often disagree, and it seems that the longer we are married and the older we get, the more the eight-year age difference is magnified. I desperately want to move back to Michigan so that I can be closer to my family, especially my grandson, but he says he will never leave North Carolina—this is one of those issues that has no solution. Although we continue to struggle with this and other concerns, we are committed to keeping our marriage covenant to each other and to God, 'til death parts us.

I am blessed with an extraordinary friendship with my mom, daughter, and sister. When we are together, it seems as if we are the only ones in the room. We know what the other is going to say even before they speak. We laugh and cry at the same time, and sometimes we laugh so hard that we wet our pants. We love the same books and often buy the same greeting cards for each other. We are kindred spirits.

I have a big, wonderful, loving family, 32 strong, that includes my husband, my children and their spouses, my grandson, my dad, Mom, four brothers, one sister, four sister-in-laws, one brother-in-law, six nephews, and eight nieces. They mean the world to me. They are:

- Joe
- Dawnie, Todd, and baby Grant (Buddy)
- Matthew and Katrina
- Daddy
- Mom

- Bumpy, Nancy, Amy, Sarah, and John Adam
- Kristen and Kevin
- Mike, Lori, Misty, and Shane
- Jeff, Mary Sue, Emily, and Seth
- Tim, Julie, Jessica, and Benjamin
- Tammy, Mark, Kryn, Kayla, and Kelsey

The words in *Ecclesiastes 4* convinced me that my family has the courage and fortitude to accomplish anything and be victorious over everything. *"Two can accomplish more than twice as much as one, for the results can be much better. If one falls, the other pulls him up; but if a man falls when he is alone, he's in trouble. And one standing alone can be attacked and defeated, but two can stand back-to-back and conquer; three is even better, for a triple-braided cord is not easily broken."*

When I was in high school, I had a necklace that held a tiny mustard seed, something small and insignificant and yet Jesus Christ thought it important enough to use as an example in *Matthew 17:20: "If ye have faith as a mustard seed, you will say to this mountain, remove hence to yonder place; and it shall remove: and nothing shall be impossible unto you."*

When I started the insurmountable task of writing this book, the words discipline and faith took on new meanings. I was responsible for the commitment and discipline of writing every word, paragraph, and chapter. There were times of discouragement, like the time I lost two chapters on my computer in the early stages of typing. When my tears turned into uncontrollable sobs, my patient husband, who at times during the writing of this book felt like he was a single man, calmly said, "You will rewrite those chapters better than ever." His unwavering faith gave me the confidence I needed to finish the task.

It disappointed me that some of my siblings weren't receptive of my book and did not want to contribute a testimony. I felt that they were coping by shoving the past deeper and deeper into the secret places of their hearts. I had to keep my eyes on my vision and respect their opinions even though I didn't agree with them.

I share my past as an incest survivor whenever I have an opportunity, and those who listen are often astounded. They can't imagine that I was a victim of sexual abuse, because I have been transformed from a frightened child into a confident, Christian woman. Sharing my story has empowered me

with incredible courage and determination to do everything I can to effect critical and necessary changes.

In 1999, Dad sent some encouraging words to me in several of his letters. He said he thought it was great that I wanted to get involved in speaking about child abuse and that I would be a real blessing to people I helped. And he told me to keep the faith and that God had a plan for me in His work that would include playing my flute. Dad seems to be making sincere attempts to keep in touch with his family, and during this past year all of my siblings have contacted him in an effort to rebuild relationships. Time heals, and for some of us, it just takes more time.

I have been blessed above and beyond anything I ever imagined, and some of these blessings are almost impossible to put into words. Being the mother of two precious children is one of those blessings. Encouraging and nurturing them, watching them develop and grow from dependent babies into playful children, then into confused, full-of-life teenagers, and finally, into responsible adults, has been a life-changing event for me. I am convinced beyond all doubt that being a mother is the most incredibly awesome and rewarding thing I will ever do in my life.

My son, Matthew, a just man who walks in integrity, graduated from law school in May, 2000, and passed the North Carolina Bar exam in July—two of the happiest days of my life. He began a solo law practice in May 2002, and was recently promoted to Captain in the National Guard, and is a professional trumpeter in the Charlotte Philharmonic.

My daughter-in-law, Katrina, recently graduated with her master's degree in opera at the prestigious North Carolina School of the Arts. She has the heart and voice of an angel.

My daughter, Dawnie, scored in the high 90s on the Michigan Automobile Insurance exam several years ago. She is an office manager at an insurance company in Michigan. The president of the company told me that she does an exemplary job and that he didn't know if he could ever replace her. Her high standard and excellent service have won her the loyalty and respect of clients and peers alike. She has taught me many valuable lessons. Her husband, Todd, graduated with honors from Drill Instructor School in Lansing, Michigan, and is an instructor with the Michigan Department of Corrections. He has made our daughter very happy.

I finally purchased my first professional model sterling silver flute—it is my most prized material possession.

Dawnie finally got her Cabbage Patch doll, and on Thursday, November

9, 2001, she gave birth to her first child and my first grandchild, Grant (Buddy) Alexander Pickett. In only a few short months, Buddy has brought unimaginable joy, happiness, and love to everyone in our family. He is a precious gift from Heaven. Truly, God is faithful!

Twenty-Six

The Future

Lilacs have always been and continue to be a symbol of beauty and hope for me. When I was a little girl, the lilacs could almost make me forget my grief. When my mom and my sister's family came to visit me two years ago, they brought me five lilac bushes from Michigan—my niece Kayla's idea. The next morning they were carefully planted in our yard. Each day, as I lovingly nurture and water these treasures from "home," the memories of the beautiful lilacs at 522 Pipestone Road deluge my heart and soul. As I watch them grow bigger and stronger, I too become stronger emotionally, mentally, and physically.

The tragedies in my life have increased my faith tremendously and have put me in a position where I have had to trust God and those who love me—what an awesome and secure place to be. As Pastor Alan Wright wrote in his endorsement, "The misery of my painful past will soon become the ministry of my future."

I am once again soaring high above anyone or anything that can hurt me, only this time I'm holding my Heavenly Father's hand. I am His special little girl.

EPILOGUE

On Saturday, February 1, 2003, at approximately 10:30 in the evening, Daddy was found alone in his prison cell, dead. Once again, my soul was crushed. I cried uncontrollably throughout the night, until the first promise of sunlight appeared through the clouds. Forgiveness had taken place long ago, and I loved him dearly. Although grieving, I am thankful for the assurance that he is in the arms of God. At heaven's gates, I envisioned my Heavenly Father handing Jody Lynn to Daddy as He spoke the gentle, caring words, "Here's your baby daughter John—she's been waiting for you." Someday, I will see my daddy again.

From my youngest brother Timmy: My father had two sides. The side of him that brings joy and encouragement to my soul is the man that I loved, the charismatic, compassionate, fun loving man that wanted to make time for his family and friends. My most precious memory is when Dad led me to Jesus at the tender age of twelve—without Jesus in my life, I would be a flower without sun. My father's other side was the repulsive, worldly side that gave in to his own selfish desires. The guilt devoured him emotionally and physically, ultimately killing him. His heart wanted to do the right thing, and yet his flesh failed often. This side is now redeemed.

Dad taught me an important lesson from his grave—look at the heart, not the sin. God never gave up on my father. He looked deep into Dad's heart and softly and tenderly wooed him back to the Cross. My family and I prayed that Dad would come back to the Lord, no matter what it took. Our prayers were answered.

DOUGLAS A DROSSMAN, MD

University of North Carolina School of Medicine,
Chapel Hill, North Carolina

I am Dr. Douglas A. Drossman, MD, and I fully endorse Jody L. Rutherford's manuscript entitled *His Special Little Girl.* I have read the manuscript and found it clearly written, emotionally compelling, and stark in its detail. I believe this detail is critical and necessary in order to awaken the public about this hidden secret within society. I would like to congratulate Ms. Rutherford for her courage in candidly sharing the thoughts and feelings that emerged in her after undergoing these abusive experiences that irrevocably changed her life.

As an academic gastroenterologist with training in psychiatry, I have become very aware of the relationship of severe stress and life trauma with gastrointestinal illness and disease. This knowledge, acquired over the last 20 years, has impacted in my clinical practice and research. As a clinician I observed very early in my practice that many women who came to me with severe painful gastrointestinal complaints and abnormalities in bowel habit had previously experienced, or were concurrently undergoing physical, sexual and emotional abuse (often in combination). In this regard, it is important to note that Ms. Rutherford's recounting of childhood episodes of abdominal pain, diarrhea and constipation, and her later diagnosis of colonic inertia and pelvic flood dyssynergia are neither unique nor coincidental. Instead, these symptoms and diagnoses reflect the common experience that I have observed among many of the women who have come to see me, and who in fact were also victims of abuse.

My research on the impact of abuse on gastrointestinal illness and its clinical outcome was a logical extension of these clinical observations. It was a means to understand and validate my clinical findings, and to learn more about how to best treat patients with such difficulties. We first undertook a survey of all the women coming to the gastroenterology clinic at the University of North Carolina asking about abuse history. We published in

184

1990 (1) that 44% of the women had been physically or sexually abused in childhood or adulthood, and in only 17% of the women so abused, was this knowledge known to the physician. We were then fortunate to acquire a large research grant from the National Institutes of Health, and through this research were able to report to physicians that a history of abuse is one of the most serious factors that adversely affect the psychological and physical health of women with gastrointestinal complaints (2-5) (6).

Over the last decade, this knowledge has become widely accepted, verified and in fact legitimized, by other investigators both nationally (7) and internationally (8). We have also learned that the effects of abuse can impact on many other medical conditions (9;10). It is now time for the general public to be aware that the health consequences of these unwanted and hidden experiences are universal and profound, and they extend way beyond the emotional distress that is commonly recognized.

I believe that Ms. Rutherford's story of victimization, conflict and confrontation, resolution and healing is an accurate portrayal of what victims of abuse need to go through in order to become re-empowered and whole again. Unfortunately, this occurs all too infrequently because society chooses to hide what is shameful. Hopefully, Ms. Rutherford's story will open up a more minds.

Sincerely,

Douglas A. Drossman, MD
Professor of Medicine and Psychiatry

Reference List

(1) Drossman DA, Leserman J, Nachman G, Li Z, Gluck H, Toomey TC et al. Sexual and physical abuse in women with functional or organic gastrointestinal disorders. Ann Intern Med. 1990;113:828-33.

(2) Leserman J, Drossman DA, Li Z, Toomey TC, Nachman G, Glogau L. Sexual and physical abuse in gastroenterology practice: How types of abuse impact health status. Psychosom Med. 1996;58:4-15.

(3) Drossman DA, Li Z, Leserman J, Toomey TC, Hu Y. Health status by gastrointestinal diagnosis and abuse history. Gastroenterol. 1996;110:999-1007.

(4) Leserman J, Toomey TC, Drossman DA. Medical consequences of sexual and physical abuse in women. Humane Med. 1995;11:23-28.

(5) Leserman J, Li Z, Drossman DA, Toomey TC, Nachman G, Glogau L. Impact of sexual and physical abuse dimensions on health status: Development of an abuse severity measure: Development of an abuse severity measure. Psychosom Med. 1997;59:152-60.

(6) Drossman DA, Li Z, Leserman J, Keefe FJ, Hu YJ, Toomey TC. Effects of coping on health outcome among female patients with gastrointestinal disorders. Psychosom Med. 2000;62:309-17.

(7) Drossman DA, Talley NJ, Olden KW, Leserman J, Barreiro MA. Sexual and physical abuse and gastrointestinal illness: Review and recommendations. Ann Intern Med. 1995;123:782-94.

(8) Drossman DA. Irritable Bowel Syndrome and Sexual/Physical Abuse History. Eur J Gastroenterol & Hepatol. 1997;9:327-30.

(9) Laws A. Sexual abuse history and women's medical problems. J Gen Intern Med. 1993;8:441-43.

(10) Laws A. Does a History of Sexual Abuse in Childhood Play a Role in Women's Medical Problems? A Review. Journal of Women's Health. 1993;2:165-72.

NATIONAL CHILD VICTIMIZATION INFORMATION – 2000

National Clearinghouse on Child Abuse and Neglect (NCANDS)
Washington, D.C.
www.calib.com/nccanch

NCANDS was developed by the Children's Bureau of the U.S. Department of Human Services in partnership with the states to collect annual statistics on child maltreatment from state child protective service agencies. The following summary of key findings presents highlights based on data submissions by the states for the calendar year 2000:

In 2000, three million referrals concerning the welfare of approximately five million children were made to child protection agencies throughout the U.S. Professionals, including teachers, law enforcement officers, social service workers, and physicians, made more than half (56%) of the screened-in reports. Others, including family members, neighbors, and other members of the community, made the remaining screened-in referrals (44%). Approximately 879,000 children were found to be victims of child maltreatment. Almost two-thirds of child victims (63%) suffered neglect (including medical neglect); 19% were physically abused, 10% were sexually abused, and 8% were psychologically maltreated.

Sixty percent (60%) of perpetrators were females, and 40% were males. The median age of female perpetrators was 31 years, and the median age of male perpetrators was 34 years. More than 80% of victims (84%) were abused by a parent or parents.

CHILD ABUSE FACTS AND INFORMATION

www.ccfh-nc.medem.com

American Medical Association

Child abuse is a much bigger problem than many people realize, and many of you may know or suspect a child who is being abused. Although many parents fear the unknown molester, a child is actually much more likely to be abused by someone they know. An abuser can be anyone caring for a child: a parent or other relative, a baby-sitter, a teacher, a neighbor or a friend. There is no typical child abuser. People who abuse children come from all backgrounds, men and women can be abusers, and even older children adolescents can be abusers.

There are certain characteristics that are risk factors for child abuse. Some of these are:

- Other violence in the home.
- Alcohol or other drug abuse by parents or caretakers.
- Parental depression or mental illness.
- Family stress due to job loss, financial burdens, illness, death, separation, or divorce.
- Adult member(s) of the family who were themselves abused as children.

Warning signs of abuse

Children will not always tell when they have been or are being abused. Sometimes they are threatened or coerced by the abuser and may fear that the abuse will become worse or more frequent if they tell. Children who are raised in an abusive household may see the abuse as normal. It is up to an adult to recognize that a child is in an abusive situation. Some signs that may indicate child abuse include:

- A poor self-image.
- Sexual acting out.
- Anger and rage.
- Passive or withdrawn behavior.
- Drug or alcohol abuse.
- Change in behavior or school performance.
- Unexplained bruises.
- Very demanding or very obedient.
- Aggressive, disruptive, and sometimes illegal behavior.
- Nightmares or problems sleeping.
- Depression, sadness, frequent crying or lying.
- Fear of certain persons or places.
- Unreasonable fear of a physical exam.
- Create drawings that show sexual acts or that seem overly focused on body parts (e.g., genitals, breasts, mouth, anus).
- Preoccupation with or overly concerned about genitals and sexual acts and words.
- Wetting the bed long after the child has been potty trained.

Consequences and effects of abuse

Child abuse has very real long-term effects on an individual. Damage done to children can haunt them in many ways for the rest of their lives. Compared with non-abused children, children who are abused are more likely to become victims of abuse later in life, are more likely to become abusers, and are more likely to be involved in violent criminal activity in the future.

Adults who were abused as children often have medical problems, including chronic pain, abdominal complaints, musculoskeletal complaints, asthma or other respiratory ailments, obesity and eating disorders, insomnia, sexual dysfunction, and neurological symptoms such as dizziness. They may also suffer from depression, self-destructive behavior, and suicide attempts.

How and what to teach your children

- Talk to your children about abuse.
- Teach them that nobody has the right to hurt them or touch them where

they don't want to be touched.
- Explain the "bathing suit rule": Nobody but a doctor during a physical exam should touch them in a place that a bathing suit covers. Many parents now accompany their children into the examination room and remain there throughout the exam.
- Be open to your child's questions about abuse and be sure to listen when your child is trying to tell you something.

American Academy of Pediatrics
www.ccfh-nc.medem.com

If the abuser is a friend or family member, you may be tempted to try to solve the problem yourself. However, when parents try to stop sexual abuse themselves, they will almost always be unsuccessful. The hard but healthy way to deal with this problem is:

- Face the issue.
- Take charge of the situation.
- Confront the problem to avoid future abuse.
- Discuss the problem with your pediatrician who can provide support and counseling.
- Report abuse to your local child protection service agency and ask about crisis support help.

Age	Prevention Plan
18 Months	Teach your child the proper names for body parts.
3-5 Years	Teach your child about "private parts" of the body and how to say "no" to sexual advances. Give straightforward answers about sex.
5-8 Years	Discuss safety away from home and the difference between being touched in private parts of the body and other touching.
8-12 Years	Stress personal safety and give examples of possible problem areas, such as video arcades, malls, locker rooms, and out-of-the-way places. Start to discuss rules of sexual conduct that are not accepted by the family.
13-18 Years	Re-stress personal safety and potential problem areas. Discuss rape, date rape, sexually transmitted diseases, and pregnancy.

U.S. Department of Health & Human Services (HHS)
www.nccanch@calib.com

The number of maltreated children in American remains unacceptably high and stands as an affront and a challenge to all of us. Behind the statistics are real children who are suffering real physical and emotional pain. We're pleased that child abuse is down significantly in the past decade, but we must continue to strive to eliminate the mistreatment of children from our society.

- It is shameful and startling to see that so many more children are in danger and that proportionately fewer incidents are investigated. Now states, schools, health-care professional—all of us—must commit ourselves to investigating and preventing child abuse with far greater effectiveness than we have seen in the past.
- Schools identified the largest number of children at risk, yet state services investigated only 16% of these children. For the cases identified in the study, less than 50% of children identified as maltreated by any source (except law enforcement) were investigated by child protective services.
- We are giving states more flexibility, demanding more accountability and focusing on the only bottom line that matters: results.
- Girls are sexually abused three times more often than boys.

U.S. Department of Justice, Bureau of Justice Statistics, 1997

- Every 15 seconds another child is sexually abused. Most perpetrators have at least 171 victims. There are currently 60 million survivors of child abuse in the United States today.
- On a given day in 1994 there were approximately 234,000 offenders convicted of rape or sexual assault under the care, custody, or control of corrections agencies; nearly 60% of these sex offenders are under conditional supervision in the community.
- The median age of the victims of imprisoned sexual assaulters was less than 13 years old; the median age of rape victims was about 22 years old.
- An estimated 24% of those serving time for rape and 19% of those serving time for sexual assault had been on probation or parole at the time of the offense for which they were in state prison in 1991.

- Offenders who had victimized a child were on average five years older than the violent offenders who had committed their crimes against adults.
- Nearly 25% of child victimizers were age 40 or older, but about 10% of the inmates with adult victims fell in that age range.
- Convicted rape and sexual assault offenders serving time in state prisons report that two-thirds of their victims were under the age of 18, and 58% of those—or nearly four in 10 imprisoned violent sex offenders—said their victims were age 12 or younger.
- Sex offenders constitute 4.7% of the almost five million offenders in federal or state prisons, jails, on probation, or parole.
- Sex offenders comprise: 1% of the federal prison population, 9.7% of the state prison population, 3.4% of jail inmates, 3.6% of offenders on probation, and 4% of the offenders on parole.
- Forty-four percent of rape victims were younger than 18 years old according to data from police-recorded incidents in three states. Two-thirds of state incarcerated violent sex offenders said their victims were younger than 18. An estimated 15% of imprisoned rapists said their victims were 12 years old or younger. An estimated 45% of those sentenced to prison for other sexual assaults (statutory rape, forcible sodomy and molestation) said their victims were 12 years old or younger.
- Most imprisoned sex offenders know their victims. Among rapists, about 30% said their victims had been strangers. Of those convicted of other sexual assaults, less than 15% said the victims were people with whom they had no prior relationship.
- Of the rapes and sexual assaults reported by victims, 60% took place in the victim's home or at the home of a friend, relative or neighbor.
- Offenders who served time for sexual assault were 7.5 times as likely as those convicted of other crimes to be rearrested for a new sexual assault. Approximately 8% of 2,214 rapists released from prisons in 11 states in 1983 were rearrested for a new rape within three years, compared to approximately 1% of released prisoners who served time for robbery or assault.
- In 90% of the rapes of children less than 12 years old, the child knew the offender according to police-recorded incident date.
- An average of 5.5 children per 10,000 enrolled in day care are sexually abused.
- Forty-two percent of women and 33% of men never disclose their

experiences to anyone.
- Approximately 31% of women in prison state that they have been abused as children.
- Long-term effects of child abuse include fear, anxiety, depression, anger, hostility, inappropriate sexual behavior, poor self esteem, tendency toward substance abuse and difficult with close relationships.
- Among victims of sexual abuse, the inability to trust is pronounced which contributes to secrecy and non-disclosure.
- Children often fail to report because of the fear that disclosure will bring consequences even worse than being victimized again. Victims may be embarrassed to answer questions about the sexual abuse.
- Victims may feel that something is wrong with them and that the abuse is their fault. In addition to the sexual guild, there are several other types of guilt associated with the abuse, which include feeling different from peers, harboring vengeful and angry feelings toward both parents, and bringing disloyalty and disruption to the family. Any of these feelings could outweigh the decision to report, the result of which is the secret may remain intact and undisclosed.
- Young victims may not recognize their victimization as sexual abuse.
- Guilt is universally experienced by almost all victims—the sexual guilt is described as guilt derived from sexual pleasure.
- Sexual victimization may profoundly interfere with and alter the development of attitudes toward self, sexuality, and trusting relationships during the critical early years of development.
- Early identification of sexual abuse victims appears to be crucial to the reduction of suffering of abused youth. As long as disclosure continues to be a problem for young victims, then fear, suffering, and psychological distress, will, like the secret, remain with the victim.
- Young girls who are forced to have sex are three times more likely to develop psychiatric disorders or abuse alcohol and drugs in adulthood, than girls who are not sexually abused.
- Sexual abuse may lead some girls to become sexually active at an earlier age and seek out older boyfriends who might, in turn, introduce them to drugs.
- Among both adolescent girls and boys, a history of sexual or physical abuse appears to increase the risk of disordered eating behaviors, such as self-induced vomiting or use of laxatives to avoid gaining weight.

- About 95% of victims know their perpetrators.
- It is estimated that approximately 71% of child sex offenders are under 35 and knew the victim as least casually. About 80% of these individuals fall within normal intelligence ranges; 59% gain sexual access to their victims through seduction or enticement.

How to Get Help

If you or someone you know is being abused or molested in any way, tell someone. I know it takes a great deal of courage, but you can do it. If you can't tell a family member, go to someone in your church, school, or local police department OR call one of the help lines listed below. The compassionate voice at the other end of the telephone line will give you encouragement and support and guide you through the entire process of making that first step toward getting help for yourself or for someone else. Remember—your courage may save another child from being hurt.

Childhelp's National Child Abuse Hotline
800-4-A-CHILD (800-422-4453)

Child Help USA – 24-hour crisis hot line; national information and referral network.
6463 Independence Avenue
Woodland Hills, CA 91367
800-422-4453

Child Welfare League of America – 75 years old; 800 public/private non-profit agencies; plays major advocacy role on Capitol Hill; world's largest publisher of child welfare materials.
440 First Street, NW, Suite 310
Washington, DC 20001-2085
202-638-2952

High Teens Ministries – A self-help program available for parents and kids in family crises involving drugs, runaways, abuse, arrest, and others.
P.O. Box 2366
Tijeras, NM 87059
505-281-0185

National Committee to Prevent Child Abuse (NCPCA) – not-for-profit; goal is to prevent child abuse; promotes public education; chapters located

throughout U.S.
P.O. Box 2866
Chicago, IL 60690
800-556-2722

National Council on Child Abuse and Family Violence – This group's purpose is to strengthen, both professionally and financially, child abuse programs and family violence prevention and treatment programs in the United States.
National Office
Washington Square
1155 Connecticut Avenue N.W., Suite 400
Washington, DC 20036
202-429-6695
info@NCCAFV.org
http://www.nccafv.org

Parents Anonymous – This international organization is committed to the prevention and treatment of child abuse. Supportive self-help groups work to prevent parents from hurting their children by helping them to build positive relationships and reconstruct self-image.
National Office
675 W. Foothill Boulevard, Suite 220
Claremont, CA 91711
909-621-6184
parentsanon@msn.com
http://www.parentsanonymous-natl.org

Prevent Child Abuse America – This organization promotes healthy parenting and community involvement as effective strategies for preventing all forms of child abuse.
200 S. Michigan Avenue, 17th Floor
Chicago, IL 60624
800-CHILDREN
mailbox@preventchildabuse.org
www.preventchildabuse.org

Rape Abuse & Incest National Network (RAINN) – A national network of rape crisis centers. This is an automated service that links callers to the nearest

rape crisis center automatically
800-656-4673 (HOPE)

SCAN – Stop Child Abuse Now
Exchange Club Child Abuse Prevention Center of North Carolina
Dorothy Walker, MS, NCC, LPC – Director, Sexual Offender Treatment
Program
500 W. Northwest Boulevard
Winston-Salem, NC 27105
336-748-9028
scan@nr.infi.net

CAREACT of 1999

www.careact.org

In most states, the penalty for an adult who rapes a child is 20 years plus—UNLESS that adult happens to be related to the child—in which case the maximum sentence could be PROBATION. In many states, including North Carolina, a stranger who rapes a child can get 12 years to life in prison— if the same monster rapes his own child or niece, he/she could be charged with misdemeanor incest and walk away with probation and a social worker. Such archaic laws don't get much more depraved.

If Congress passes the bill into law, the CAREACT will change all of this. IF YOU CARE, notify your state representatives and tell them that you want to see the CAREACT reintroduced. Or, you may send an email to Congressman Robert Ney's legislative assistant at brett.palmer@mail.house.gov.

Questions and Answers

What do you mean by "incest"? "Incest," also called "intrafamilial child sexual abuse, is used here to mean the sexual abuse of a child by a family member.

What is the "incest exception?" The "incest exception" is the special opportunity the law gives to certain sex offenders in most states. It allows offenders related to the victim by blood or marriage to be charged with "incest," instead of "child sexual abuse" or "rape of a child." This charge bargaining is a covert form of plea bargaining, and it can allow predators who grow their own victims to escape prison. Simply stated, the "incest exception" means an exemption from the harsh penalties generally applied to those who molest or rape a child.

A perpetrator of child sexual abuse who is not related to the child may be charged with child rape and assault and child molestation. If the perpetrator is convicted of all counts (or even just the first one), he/she could spend two decades or more in prison. And a plea, even to the lowest count, is still going

to result in prison time. In contrast, the perpetrator who is related to the child may be charged with child rape and assault and child molestation and incest. Incest with a child is a crime, but a crime that most often results in no prison time.

Most abuse cases are disposed of by plea bargain, and as long as there is a guilty plea to any count, the prosecutor counts it on his "win record," regardless of whether the perpetrator spends any time behind bars. Prosecutors are elected officials who remain in office by presenting their success at garnering guilty pleas and convictions for crimes. The "incest exception" flourishes because prosecutors are elected on the basis of their conviction rates without regard to the actual sentences handed out to criminals. As a result of a plea bargain to an incest charge, the intrafamilial abuser escapes prison time and reenters the community, the prosecutor has another success on his record, and everyone but the victim wins. But our whole society loses.

Most people have no idea that this disparity exists. We all want strict child sexual abuse laws—40 states have laws that penalize the top count of sexually abusing a child with significant prison time. But the existence of the "incest exception" makes a mockery of that strict penalty when the victim is related to, or as many offenders would claim, "owned by" the perpetrator. This was never the will of the American people, the vast majority of whom see the rape of one's own child as an even more despicable crime.

What will the CAREACT do? It will eliminate this wrongful grant of prosecutorial discretion, and prosecutors will no longer be able to offer any perpetrator a chance to bargain to an incest count that excludes prison time altogether. If the bill passes, it will create hope (which is a wonderful thing in itself). It will also change the way the so-called "system" protects predators from their just punishment and help protect the community from continuing crimes. Most importantly, it will prove to America's children that we care enough about them to protect them by law.

What else will the CAREACT do? The CAREACT will direct every state to begin recording the number of child rapes and sex assaults; the perpetrators arrested, convicted, and sentenced; and the relationship of the perpetrator to the victim. The information will go to the U.S. Department of Justice, which must publicly report every year. This sort of record keeping has never been done before, and it will throw a revealing spotlight on a vicious crime that everyone abhors but no one has ever been able to quantify with any statistical certainty.

Supporters of the CAREACT do not claim that no perpetrators ever do

any prison time for raping their own children. This is not about statistics, it is about opportunity—a wrongful opportunity for the worst offenders. The very existence of the "incest exception" is odious. To defend its existence, one must be willing to take the position that a child is injured LESS when the rapist (the molester or abuser) is the same adult whom the community believes should be the child's best protector.

There is no doubt that this foul discount remains available in the majority of America's states, and any person who claims to care about protecting children must do his or her part to erase its availability. If you know any reporters or have any suggestions for local newspapers, television, or radio stations in your area that would be willing to do a story, please ask them to contact us. We have press releases about the fact that this is the first federal bill with its own dedicated web site, a point of interest for technology and cyber-news reporters everywhere.

If our friends and supporters stand with us, then we will win this fight. As vocal citizens, we possess true, collective power to force change. Until there is finally a special interest group for children, Americans will be seen as the worst of hypocrites, telling the world that we prize our children above all else, but allowing special, lenient treatment for those who violate their own.

RECOMMENDED READINGS

- *A Betrayal of Innocence*, by David Peters, Word Inc.
- *A Door of Hope*, by Jan Frank, Here's Life Publishers
- *A House Divided*, by Kathryn Edwards, Zondervan
- *As Jesus Cared for Women*, by Dr. W. David Hager, Fleming H. Revell
- *Beauty for Ashes: Receiving Emotional Healing*, by Joyce Meyer
- *Daddy Loves His Girls*, by Rev. T. D. Jakes,
- *False Intimacy*, by Harry W. Schaumburg, Navpress
- *Father Hunger*, by Robert S. McGee, Servant
- *Healing for Damaged Emotions*, by Dr. David Seamands, Victor Publishing
- *Healing of Memories*, by David Seamands, Victor Books
- *Healing Victims of Sexual Abuse*, by Paula Sandford, Victory House
- *I Should Forgive, But...*, by Dr. Charles Lynch, Word Inc.
- *Lives on the Mind*, by Florence Littauer, Word Inc.
- *Out of the Shadows*, by Patrick J. Carnes, CompCare
- *Putting Your Past Behind You*, by Edwin W. Lutzer, Moody Press
- *Sexual Assault, by Kay Scott*, Bethany
- *Sexual Healing*, by David Kyle Foster, Privately Published
- *Something Must Be Wrong with Me*, by Doris Sanford, Multnomah/Questar
- *The Princess Within*, by Serita Ann Jakes, Albury Publishing
- *The Father Heart of God*, by Floyd McClung, Jr., Harvest House
- *The Wounded Heart*, by Dr. Dan B. Allender, NavPress
- *Growing Beyond Survival: A Self-Help Toolkit for Managing Traumatic Stress,* by Elizabeth Vermilyea, Sidran Press
- *Trauma and Recovery,* by Judith L. Herman, Basic Books
- *Legacy of the Heart: The Spiritual Advantages of a Painful Childhood,* by Wayne Muller, Fireside Books

RECOMMENDED MUSIC

- *He is Still a Father*, Words by Ray Boltz and Steve Millikan, Sung by Priscilla Engle

RECOMMENDED WEB SITES

- www.njprotectthechildren.org Protect the Children, A non profit organization formed in order to change the current penalties for convicted child molesters to that they serve life in prison without the possibility of parole
- www.prevent-abuse-now.com/index.htm Sexual Abuse features more than 200 articles about identifying child sexual abuse, reporting it, and recovering from the trauma.
- www.childlures.com/ Child Lures program has been keeping children safe from sexual abuse and abduction for over fifteen years.
- www.ncjrs.org/txtfiles/exploit.txt Child Sexual Exploitation: Improving and protecting Victims
- www.calib.com/nccanch/pubs/usermanuals/crisis/index.cfm Crisis Intervention in Child Abuse and Neglect
- www.breakingthesilence.com/ Breaking The Silence
- www.hc-sc.gc.ca/hppb/familyviolence/html/invisible.htm The Invisible Boy
- www.jimhopper.com/memory/ Recovered Memories of Sexual Abuse.
- www.somebodysdaughter.org Somebody's Daughter – Somebody's Son
- www.daniel-trust-ministries.org/abuse/index.html Child Sexual Abuse
- www.momskc.org Mothers Outraged at Molesters
- www.biocom.arizona.edu/psa/ Pediatric Sexual Abuse: The Clinician's Role
- www.vnh.org/NGB/HW9615ChldSexAbuse.html Protect Your Child from Sexual Abuse
- www.members.aol.com/kevinscull/ache/1998.html Action on Child Exploitation
- www.geocities.com/HotSprings/Chalet/3432/index.html Effects of Child Sexual Abuse Upon Victims
- www.angelfire.com/tx4/childprotection/ Child Protection, Describes stages of grief observed in parents who are dealing with the sexual abuse of their child.

- www.hearthealers.org Heart Healers
- www.law.about.com/newsissues/law/cs/childsexualabuse/index.html Child Abuse Legal Issues
- www.angelfire.com/ga3/protectourkidz Protect Our Kidz - Child Molestation and Awareness
- www.drgreene.com/html/21792.html Sexual Abuse, Dr. Green discusses signs of symptoms of sexual abuse in young children, both physical and emotional
- www.polygraph.org.apa1.htm#post American Polygraph Association, Post conviction sex offender testing
- www.ncsac.org/main.html National Council on Sexual Addiction and Compulsivity, Promotes public and professional recognition, awareness and understanding of sexual addiction
- www.boards.parentsoup.com/cgi-bin/boards/psppabused Parents of Abused Children
- www.ashtree.kirion.net Through It Together, Help and advice for partners of survivors of child abuse
- www.stardrift.net/survivor/ I Have Survived
- www.geocities.com/alltheseyears1/ All These Years
- www.aest.uk6.net Abused Empowered Survivor Thrive
- www.fatherstouch.com Father's Touch, Donald D'Haene's powerful and brutally honest memoir chronicles his experience of being sexually abused for over a decade within a Jehovah's Witness family and the subsequent trial of abuser
- www.alterboys.tripod.com/Faith/Clergy_Abuse_x.html Alterboys.net
- www.silentnomore.net A Survivor's Site – Silent No More
- www.aftersilence-bynvraine.net After Silence: Rape and My Journey Back
- www.geocities.com/Wellesley/4542/ A Christian's experience with childhood sexual abuse, her healing, and her faith
- www.survivorwit.com Survivor Wit, Offers free email newsletters of humor for survivors of childhood sexual abuse and their supporters
- www.members.tripod.com/~mrs88888/index.html Not a Victim Anymore, Created for survivors to see that they are not alone
- www.angiesue.htmlplanet.com A Place of Hope, Healing, and Comfort, A survivor tells her story and how God's grace has helped her survive the dark years that followed

- www.theweepers.tripod.com My Twisted Sukha, This site deals with the affects of sexual abuse by a female perpetrator
- www.black_sheep3,tripod.com/index.htm The Black Sheep Chronicles, Adult incest survivor's experiences with the aftermath of incest and how and why it affected her relationships with her entire family
- www.adultsurvivors.org Adult Survivors Anonymous, A free 10 step recovery and healing program
- www.geocities.com/ombadykow Surviving Abuse, A Christian site of support and encouragement for women who have been sexually abused
- www.members.tripod.com/~NoColluding Confronting Collusion in Churches, This site offers a source of support for survivors, church leaders, and survivor advocates struggling with clergy sexual abuse, domestic violence, and incest
- www.angelfire.lycos.com/journal/achingheart Aching Heart

BIBLIOGRAPHY

1. *The News Palladium* (later named *The Herald-Palladium*)
2. *Running for Daddy*, by Kay Arthur
3. *The Five Love Languages*, by Gary Chapman PhD., Moody Press
4. *Ludington Daily News*

To Contact the Author

You can reach Jody Rutherford confidentially at:
jodyrutherford@yahoo.com

Printed in the United States
1445900006B/117

9 781592 866977